DYING WITH JESUS

A Love Story

*"Yea, though I walk through
the valley of the shadow of death,
I will fear no evil:
for thou art with me;
Thy rod and thy staff
they comfort me."
Psalm 23:4*

by
Brenda Abell

TEACH Services, Inc.
PUBLISHING
www.TEACHServices.com • (800) 367-1844

World rights reserved. This book or any portion thereof may not be copied or reproduced in any form or manner whatever, except as provided by law, without the written permission of the publisher, except by a reviewer who may quote brief passages in a review.

The author assumes full responsibility for the accuracy of all facts and quotations as cited in this book. The opinions expressed in this book are the author's personal views and interpretations, and do not necessarily reflect those of the publisher.

This book is provided with the understanding that the publisher is not engaged in giving spiritual, legal, medical, or other professional advice. If authoritative advice is needed, the reader should seek the counsel of a competent professional.

Copyright © 2016 TEACH Services, Inc.

ISBN-13: 978-1-4796-0588-0 (Paperback)

ISBN-13: 978-1-4796-0589-7 (ePub)

ISBN-13: 978-1-4796-0590-3 (Mobi)

Library of Congress Control Number: 2016900318

Published by

www.TEACHServices.com • (800) 367-1844

A WORD OF EXPLANATION

Brenda Abell is a Seventh-day Adventist Christian who loves God deeply and believes that He communicates through His Holy Spirit—both through the biblical gift of prophecy and in the life of the believer. Along with other Seventh-day Adventists, she recognizes that God promised the gift of prophecy to the New Testament church, and she believes that Mrs. Ellen G. White possessed that gift. (See the tests of a prophet in Matt. 24:24; 7:16, 20; 1 John 4:1–3; Isa. 8:20; Jer. 28:9; and Deut. 13:1–4.) In recounting her journey, Mrs. Abell refers to specific matters of diet outlined by Mrs. White, as well as Mrs. White's counsel for families to move out of large cities. She also refers to a "medical missionary," by which she means an individual who ministers to spiritual needs by ministering to a person's physical health. In this case, the missionary used herbs and simple hydrotherapy treatments, such as hot and cold soaks, enemas, and fomentations (which are the application of hot and cold towels to specific portions of the body).

Mrs. Abell also refers to the blessing of the seventh-day Sabbath, which was introduced by God in Genesis 2 and validated by Jesus in Mark 2, when He declared: "The Sabbath was made for man." She also mentions the covenant of tithe, which is the returning a tenth of one's financial increase. For those unfamiliar with 3ABN (the Three Angels Broadcasting Network), which Mrs. Abell also mentions, this is a nonprofit, 24-hour television and radio network that focuses primarily on Christian and health-oriented programming.

Mrs. Abell writes tenderly and candidly about the experience that she shared with her husband Lawrence. Much of what she shares comes from journals that she kept through that experience. In reading her story, we were deeply moved, and we trust that her account will move you and have a positive impact on your life as well.

THE PUBLISHERS

About the Author

Brenda Abell lives in Oroville, northern California, where she owns and operates a care home for the elderly. She believes firmly that all things work together for good for those who love God. She enjoys entertaining, spending time with family and friends, and serving others. She loves to tease, to laugh, and to make jokes. She believes that the Holy Spirit guides those who are open to His leading.

Dedicated to Lora Hairston- Abell.
Thank you for your support and help with this project. The fact that you would be willing to share this journey, though difficult I know it must have been, with Lawrence and me, is a testament that Christ has repaired the damage that we made and has brought our lives full circle. Christ prayed "Holy Father, keep through thine own name those whom thou hast given me, that they may be one, as we are one." Our hearts have come together at the foot of Christ.

*Dedicated also to my mother
for the precious gift of introducing me to God,
and raising me in a home where His presence was felt.*

INTRODUCTION

While coming home from Southern to Northern California, I heard the Spirit telling me to write down the account of the journey that my husband and I had begun. The title that came to me to describe our journey is: "Dying with Jesus." I had to wonder why He wanted that title. At the time, my husband had been recently diagnosed with stage-four cancer in the small bowel and the liver. However, we were praying for healing. We were *claiming* healing. We were *expecting* healing. So I asked God why He was telling me to title our journey, "Dying with Jesus."

The Spirit's answer was: *You do not know how this journey will end. Even though you are claiming and expecting healing, the journey is not about physical death.* The Spirit made plain that all humans are dying. Every one of us is on a journey that will end in the death of our physical body. However, for those who choose life with Christ, there should also be a death to self. The journey my husband and I had begun was a journey of complete and utter surrender to God. It was prompted by the circumstances that God allowed in our lives. In obedience to the prompting of the Holy Spirit, I have written down the account of that journey, and it is that journey that I wish to share with you.

CHAPTER 1. *How Our Journey Began*

It was in January of 2012 that my husband and I were at his mother's house having dinner with the rest of the family. Lawrence's brother Steven and his wife Mary had come into town for a few days in honor of Lawrence's mother's birthday. Our general custom had been to gather for a meal, and, most times, it has been at the house of my mother-in-law.

After sharing a good meal, we like to sit around the table and talk. Lawrence and his brothers find themselves teasing each other about things that happened during their childhood. Then we spend time bringing each other up on what has been going on in our lives. The men seem to always end up in a spiritual "conversation" (actually, a debate *smile*).

However, this time something different occurred. In the middle of our talking about nothing in particular, the conversation went to health. I am not sure how it started because I was having a separate conversation with my sisters-in-law. However, I remember tuning in when I heard my husband mentioning concerns he had about his health.

Lawrence is a very private man. For him to mention his health means that he must really be concerned. He told his family, "I did not think I would live past December of 2011." Then, he went on to state that he was having some symptoms. He never really said what the symptoms were. However, he stated a few times that he was surprised to still be alive in January of 2012.

Needless to say, we all sat up and took notice. The family began to ask questions, but we never could get him to be very specific. Eventually, Lawrence downplayed his comment, saying, "I always like to prepare myself for the worst. That way, when it is not as bad as I had expected, I am pleasantly surprised." The family dropped the matter, and we went on with our usual conversation.

When we got home that evening, I told my husband that I was very surprised by what he said to his family, and I asked him why he had not said anything about it to me. It is true that he had mentioned a few times that year that he was not feeling well. Yet, he had never directly or specifically told me what he was experiencing. I had no idea that he had expected to be dead by the end of the year!

Lawrence explained that he was afraid that either his colon cancer had returned or that his problem with his prostate had become cancer and had begun to metastasize. You see, back in 2005, my husband was taken in for emergency surgery to remove cancer from his colon that we discovered while vacationing in Hawaii. God blessed him in the surgery, and the surgeons were able to remove all of the cancer, with no sign of cancer in the surrounding lymph nodes. Just before the diagnosis of colon cancer, my husband had an elevated PSA, so his primary care doctor sent him to a urologist, and the urologist told him that he palpated some hardening in his prostate. The urologist wanted to do a biopsy, but Lawrence refused the procedure. The urologist reassured my husband that prostate cancer is generally very slow growing and that he would probably die of something else before the prostate cancer would get him. With this news, Lawrence decided to just watch and wait.

Let me pause here for a moment and address the men reading this: Watching and waiting is never the thing to do. It should not be an option. Wives, please insist that your husbands take action if they are experiencing any symptoms. As you continue reading, you will understand why I say this.

Chapter 1. How Our Journey Began

I told Lawrence that I was going to make an appointment with his doctor immediately. After several blood tests and bone and CT scans, the doctors confirmed the worst—Lawrence's PSA was up to 279. This signified that it was cancer even without a biopsy. Nonetheless, a biopsy was needed to determine how aggressive the cancer was. The hospital scheduled the biopsy. On the day of the scheduled procedure, Lawrence refused to go. He felt the biopsy could cause the cancer to spread, and he decided to go forward with treatment without a biopsy.

Looking back on that day, I truly feel that it was the first of many ways in which the Holy Spirit began to tenderly prepare us (and the rest of Lawrence's family) for what was ahead. You see, that night, when we got home from his mother's, I asked Lawrence what made him decide to say something to his family. His response was that he did not know; it just came out. As Christians, we know that there are no mere coincidences. We serve a God who has a plan for our lives, and, when we submit to Him, we can have confidence that He is in control.

After we received the diagnosis from Lawrence's doctor, Lawrence began to research the types of treatments that were available for prostate cancer. We heard from two different church members about the proton treatments offered at the Loma Linda Medical Center in Loma Linda, California. Loma Linda has an extremely high success rate for these treatments, with few side effects. We prayed over the decision, and the Spirit impressed us that this would be the best route for us. We submitted all of Lawrence's medical records and waited to see if he would be accepted. We were a little apprehensive, having heard that not everyone is accepted into the program. While we believed that God had led Lawrence to learn about the treatments and that God was leading him to apply, we did not know how God was working for us at that time. That knowledge would come later. After a short while, we received a call informing us that Lawrence had been accepted into the program, and we received word that he had been cleared by his insurance company for the proton treatments.

God's Miraculous Provision of Housing

Being accepted into the program meant that we would have to stay in Loma Linda for two to three months and would need to live nearby. That would have been a problem, but let me share with you how our great God worked the housing situation out for us.

Ten years before, God brought us to Oroville, California, where we found a very special group of people at the Oroville Seventh-day Adventist Church. These people have become very special to us. We are truly like a family. Knowing how loving they are, it was no surprise to us that offers of support and help came from several within the church. Once the members learned that we would need to stay in Loma Linda for several months, a dear friend of mine from church offered to make arrangements for Lawrence and I to stay with a friend or family member while we were in Loma Linda. Another dear friend, who is not a member of our church, offered to make arrangements for us to stay with a friend of hers, who lived between thirty and forty minutes from Loma Linda. However, after our first visit with the doctor at Loma Linda, we recognized that Lawrence would have to be available for his treatments at various hours of the day. Sometimes he would need to be at the hospital very early in the morning. For this reason, we felt it best that we stay close to the hospital. Though we were just finding this out, our God, who has all knowledge, saw ahead and had already made a way for us. Here is how that happened:

Lawrence and I own a care home for the elderly. For over a year, we had had a space available for a male resident. Yet, we could not find one to fill the bed. With that shortage of clients, we made enough to cover expenses but not much more.

At the beginning of the year, I had an opportunity to get a large supply of disposable underpants. I knew I could not use them all, but I was impressed by the Holy Spirit to get them and to check with some of the other care homes in my town to see if they needed any. I contacted one particular care home, and they told me that they did want some.

When I went to deliver the underpants, the owner asked me if I had an opening for a male resident. I told him that I did, and he replied, "I have a man for you." Within a couple of weeks, the man moved into our care home. Because Lawrence and I had been meeting all of our regular expenses, we felt impressed to put the money in the bank and not use it. Actually, it was Lawrence who was impressed that we should put the money in the bank. I wanted to do some work around the care home that would have been very costly, and I thought that we could charge it and then pay off the charge card with the money from the resident. Lawrence would not agree to this plan. He believed that we should save up the money from the resident until we had enough for the work. I chose to follow my husband's leading. You see, ladies, it does pay to listen to our husbands! (*Smile*)

God knew that we would need that money for what was ahead of us. Five months later, we were faced with the big financial need in going to Loma Linda, and the money was waiting for us in the bank. We would not have been able to afford treatment without going into major debt if God, in His infinite wisdom and mercy, had not provided for us before we knew that we would need it. "And it shall come to pass, that before they call, I will answer; and while they are yet speaking, I will hear" (Isaiah 65:24). This is why Lawrence and I have the confidence to put our lives into the hands of Jesus, for He tells us: "Verily, verily, I say unto you, He that believeth on me . . . whatsoever ye shall ask in my name, that will I do, that the Father may be glorified in the Son. If ye shall ask any thing in my name, I will do it" (John 14:12). This promise is broad and deep—we can hang our lives on it. The key to claiming it is in *always* praying according to God's will in total faith and confidence. In the Bible, God uses the words "believe" and "obedience" interchangeably. You will find an example of this in Numbers 20:7–12. In this passage, God gave Moses instructions to take his rod, the symbol of God's authority, and call the people together. Then Moses was to speak to the rock, and it would give forth water. Moses became upset with the people, and he and Aaron called out, "Hear now, ye rebels; must we fetch you water out of this rock?" (Num. 20:10). Then Moses hit the rock twice instead of speaking to the rock, as God had commanded him. He made it appear as if he and Aaron were the ones who were leading the people through the wilderness and not God. God told Moses, "Because ye believed me not, to sanctify me in the eyes of the children of Israel, therefore ye shall not bring this congregation into the land which I have given them" (Num. 20:12). Notice that God did not say that their exclusion from the promised land was because they did not *obey* Him; it was because they did not *believe* Him. However, when God calls upon us to *believe* Him, He expects that we will also *obey* Him. When we believe God, we obey Him. Belief and obedience go together. (See also 1 Peter 2:7 and John 3:36.) Of course, the way that we learn what God wants us to do—what He considers obedience—is from studying His Word, the Bible.

Excuse me if I digress in sharing what I have learned through God's goodness. The point of what I am saying is this: Because God had provided for a need that we did not know we would have, we were able to rent a lovely furnished apartment less than five minutes from the hospital. After we considered a few different places that we thought suitable, God led us to just the right one. Meeting with Kathleen, one of the leasing managers, we found that she too loved the Lord, and we were completely confident that this was where God would have us stay.

CHAPTER 2. *Feeling Jesus Close*

In our first consultation at Loma Linda, the doctor found out that Lawrence had refused to have a colonoscopy and a biopsy. He informed Lawrence that he would not begin treatment until Lawrence had both procedures done. I remember Lawrence commenting that he knew that he was in this situation because he had put off something that he knew needed his attention. He recognized that procrastination was one of his problems. Of course, I already knew this. If possible, Lawrence would put things off until later, and then later would never come. The doctor informed us that, because the prostate cancer was so advanced, Lawrence would need an additional twenty treatments of regular radiation besides the usual twenty proton treatments. Lawrence felt that God was teaching him by making him do everything that he had put off. He was right, and there were two applications of learning in the situation—both earthly and spiritual. On the earthly level, we realized that we needed to deal with situations no matter how difficult they might be. Whenever we put things off, they only tend to get worse.

I once heard it said that, while we feel illness is bad and unwanted, it is part of God's design. In His infinite wisdom, He created our bodies to set off alarms. When the alarms go off, that is, when illnesses happen, it is a signal to us to seek treatment, to get help and make changes. If the alarms did not go off and the illness did not occur, we would simply drop dead one day without any warning. We should welcome the alarms of illness and seek wisdom from on high through prayer for direction in dealing with illness, be it through following the divinely inspired health message or through medical intervention. We should do all that we can do to prevent illness from occurring. Yet, if illness does occur, we must seek medical help. God has given man knowledge for treating illnesses.

On a spiritual level, sin destroys and results in eternal death. We all have sins that we have allowed to find a home in us, some of which we are fully aware of and yet we find reasons for holding near. We ignore the effects that we see sin having on our life and on the lives of others. Time passes—sometimes even years may go by—and we look up to see the lives that have been destroyed through our sins. Most of the time, these sins are what we consider small sins: the lust of the eye (such as what we watch on television) and the lust of appetite. We may not trust that our God will provide for us, so we steal from God by using His tithe. We may destroy one another's characters by ill speaking. All of these sins, if left unattended, will destroy others and us. God was teaching us that putting off what should be done today will only lead to more serious problems and ultimately to death.

God showed Lawrence that, in an effort to live, he must deal with the problem. He could not get around doing what was needed, no matter how uncomfortable or painful it might be. Removal of sin from our lives depends on our willingness. Victory over sin will always be accompanied by discomfort. If sin were not enjoyable, we would not partake of it. In order to remove it from our lives, we will feel some discomfort at the least. In most cases, there will be actual pain. Yet, we serve a God who has not left us alone. He will carry us through if we will only lay our sins and pain at His feet and surrender our will to Him. He will do the work of cleansing us. "What God hath cleansed, that call not thou common" (Acts 10:15). Yet, for cleansing to occur, we must also surrender completely. "Submit yourselves therefore to God. Resist the devil, and he will flee from you" (James 4:7).

On May 22, 2012, Lawrence began treatment for prostate cancer. As we began, things went very well. The treatments were so simple. We went in for about 15–30 minutes a day for the treatment, and the rest of the time was ours. Lawrence had no side effects from the treatment, so we enjoyed spending time together. We almost felt guilty for having such a nice time. I say "almost."

During the first several weeks at Loma Linda, Lawrence and I found ourselves talking about the goodness of God. We felt Him so close to us. He had made a way for us to go to Loma Linda. He had led us to a most beautiful housing complex. Because we were in Loma Linda, California, we were surrounded by people who believed as we do. We could walk into any store and find a variety of vegetarian products. The hospital cafeteria served no meat, so we could get delicious vegetarian food there and also in many of the local restaurants as well. We were able to get 3ABN on regular television. We felt as if we were being given a taste of what it will be like when the earth is made new after Christ returns. We felt like newlyweds. We could see God's hand moving in our lives, orchestrating the events and opening doors for us. There was such a peace about us that we could not help but comment on how we felt. I remember saying to Lawrence one day, while we were discussing God's goodness, that it was my prayer that we would be able to praise God just as much during the difficult times. Little did I know the difficult times that were just ahead of us.

It is so easy for us to give God glory and praise when things are going our way, when life seems so good. However, when Satan seeks to destroy us and cause us to be discouraged, it is only through prayer and supplication that we can see God's mercy and goodness. We must hold onto the blessings that God has given us in the past as proof that He loves us, is with us, and is working things out for our good, even if we do not see it at the time. We should respond to God with belief, obedience, and praise

> *We must hold onto the blessings that God has given us in the past as proof that He loves us.*

during our times of sorrow and discouragement. I know that it was the Holy Spirit who led me to pray such a prayer. It was the Spirit who knew what was ahead and that we would need Him to draw close to us to bring back to mind just how much mercy and love He had just shown us. Then, because our eyes had been opened to this love, we would be able to see that God was in control of the circumstances and we could trust that, if He has allowed such a thing to happen, He would be faithful to give us the strength to endure, if we would just hold on.

How precious was the gift that He gave us—time away from the daily affairs of work and family, time to bask in each other's love and company without the concerns of daily life. Six weeks God gave us to renew our love for each other and for Him. We had time to rest and to get fortified for the unknown events that lay ahead. God tells us in His Word that He will not allow anything into our lives that we cannot bear. "There hath no temptation taken you but such as is common to man: but God is faithful, who will not suffer you to be tempted above that ye are able; but will with the temptation also make a way to escape, that ye may be able to bear it" (1 Cor. 10:13). I truly believe that, because God saw what was about to take place in our lives, He began ordering events to show us that He was with us. His Spirit drew so close to us that, though we knew we were in this world, we did not feel a part of it. We felt that we were in the hands of Jesus; and we were. That brought us so much peace! It is so important for each of us to pray daily that God will open our eyes to see all of the wonderful ways in which He is guiding us and working out circumstances in our lives so that we will have the strength to enter the battle with Satan, our adversary.

> *I truly believe that, because God saw what was about to take place in our lives, He began ordering events to show us that He was with us.*

The Coming Storm

About five weeks into the treatments, Lawrence started having stomach problems, having discomfort when he ate or drank. We spoke with the doctor that was over his proton treatments, and he did not feel it had anything to do with the treatments, so he just dismissed any concern. As the weeks went on, however, the pain got worse, and we convinced the doctor that Lawrence needed to be seen for the problem. He had lost sixteen pounds, and his symptoms were not getting better. Before they could get him in to see the gastroenterologist, the pain became more severe, he started vomiting, and I had to take Lawrence to the emergency room. We spent the day there, and I do mean the day. We were there from 6:00 a.m. until midnight. Hospital staff ran several test and took x-rays, which showed that Lawrence had what appeared to be a large tumor in his small bowel. He was admitted into the hospital, where they immediately placed a tube through his nose and down his throat into his stomach to relieve the pressure that was building up. The tumor was preventing the stomach gases and food from passing through. The procedure gave Lawrence the relief he needed.

Now we had to find out the best way to deal with the blockage. Two weeks passed, during which time Lawrence had several tests, x rays, and scans. He had a team of internal medicine doctors, a team of gastrointestinal doctors, and a team of surgeons. The tumor was judged to be cancerous, so he also had a team of oncologists. When the results came in, they confirmed our worst fears—not only did Lawrence have cancer in the prostate but also in the small bowels, with several cancerous lesions in his liver as well.

My husband was very sick. The doctors gave him only one treatment option, and that was chemotherapy, which they agreed would only slow the cancer down but not cure it. Lawrence could see the handwriting on the wall and had already decided that he would place everything in God's hands. We would return home and begin following God's plan regarding diet. We knew that, if he were healed, it would be God who did it. Yet, Lawrence wanted to do all that he knew to do regarding his diet.

The doctors told us that they could do a procedure that would open up the small bowel and allow Lawrence's food to process through. This would give him temporary comfort without having a tube down his throat. Once the doctors had performed the procedure and could see that Lawrence could tolerate food again, they would release him to go home.

All went well with the procedure, and the day finally came for us to leave the hospital. It had been over five weeks that Lawrence had not been able to eat much. The last two weeks of that time he was on intravenous fluids only. As you can imagine, he was very weak. When the discharge planner made arrangements for Lawrence to go home, I requested that she also make arrangements for us to have a wheelchair. The apartment we were renting was on the third floor, and there was no elevator. We also had to park some distance from our apartment, and I felt that Lawrence would not be able to walk the distance. A nurse informed us that we could get a wheelchair, yet our insurance would only cover one wheelchair within a given period of time. If we got the wheelchair then and turned it in when we were ready to go home, we would not be able to get another one once we were back in Northern California. She did say, however, that she could arrange for us to rent a wheelchair and return it. The day of my husband's discharge was a Sabbath morning, and, as a rule, we do not buy or sell on the Sabbath. You see, Lawrence and I recognized that Christ, in His infinite mercy, has made it clear that the Sabbath was made for man and not man for the Sabbath (Mark 2:27). We also knew that Christ indicated that it is "lawful to do good on the Sabbath" (Mark 3:4). Recognizing acts of mercy on the Sabbath, Jesus said: "What man shall there be among you, that shall have one sheep, and if it fall into a pit on the sabbath day, will he not lay hold on it, and lift it out?" (Matt. 12:11). We believed that, if we had chosen to get the wheelchair, it would not have been a sin. I only mention this because I feel it important in relating the providence that God performed for us. God will always honor our efforts when they are the result of our trying to obey Him. A "man of God" told Eli the priest: "Wherefore the Lord God of Israel saith, . . . them that honour me I will honour, and they that despise me shall be lightly esteemed" (1 Sam. 2:30). God asks that we do all that we know to do that is right and then trust him to take care of the rest. He asks that we trust Him to provide that which we are not able to provide for ourselves.

Lawrence thought it over and felt that he would be able to make it up to the apartment if he could stop and rest when needed. We finally left the hospital and were on our way back to the apartment. As I rolled Lawrence through the hospital doors in the hospital's wheelchair, he looked up at me with sighs of great joy. He thought for a moment and then said, "I thank God for letting me out of here." He had not been sure that he would ever see outside the hospital again. He knew how sick he was, but his prayer was that God would let him return home. We both thanked God for the mercy He had just shown us.

God loves us, and His desire is to give us that which is for our good. He promises: "Delight thyself also in the Lord; and he shall give thee the desires of thine heart" (Psalm 37:4). In His mercy, God granted my husband's desire. He knew just how much it meant to Lawrence to return home.

We had decided that Lawrence would use the fold-up chair in the trunk of our car whenever he needed to stop and rest while walking up to the apartment. As you can imagine, we only made it a short distance before Lawrence needed to use it. He sat for a while and then let me know that he would not be able to continue. I told Lawrence that I would check with the office to see if they had a wheelchair. We were renting an apartment in a senior building. Can you believe that? I was living in a *senior* building. I spent a night there and I became a "senior"! (*Smile*) I had hoped they kept a wheelchair on hand for emergencies. When I asked about the wheelchair, the office worker told me that they did not have one. I returned to Lawrence and found him talking to a man I had not seen before. He said that the man had stopped to say "hello." Lawrence and I had been at this apartment for almost two months, and we had never seen the man before. Some would say that it was just a coincidence that the man was walking by at the very moment my husband needed help, but those of us who know and appreciate our wonderful God know that that was not the case. I told Lawrence that I could not find a wheelchair. The man immediately said, "Wait here. I will be right back." He returned with a wheelchair that belonged to his roommate. He wheeled my husband up to our apartment and told us to let him know when we were ready to leave so that he could come and take Lawrence to the car. Just as God provided the ram in the bush for Abraham (Genesis 22), so did He provide a man with a wheelchair for us. He was honoring our commitment to keep the fourth commandment by not renting a wheelchair on the Sabbath, however foolish our decision might seem. God knew that Lawrence's intent was to please Him. We serve a loving and merciful God who only wants good for us. He asks that we only surrender our will to Him, and He will do the rest. Paul wrote: "I die daily" (1 Cor. 15:31). He also wrote: "And we know that all things work together for good to them that love God, to them who are the called according to His purpose" (Rom. 8:28). If we surrender our heart and will to God, dying daily, we can trust Him to work everything out for our good.

Lawrence and I had no doubt that it was the Lord God who sent that dear man to rescue us. It gave us another opportunity to see that God was with us. Although things were looking very dim, God had not abandoned us. We could trust that, no matter how things turned out, they would be for our good and our heavenly Father would be glorified.

Returning Home

Lawrence's two brothers, Rufus and Willie, along with their mother and stepfather and Rufus's wife, Shirley, drove down to be with us. They did not want us to make the long trip home alone. I am not sure if they will ever know just how much their expression of love meant to the two of us.

Lawrence was able to find a comfortable position traveling in the car. He slept most of the way home, while Willie and I drove. It was on this trip home that the Holy Spirit told me that He wanted me to write down all the events that had and were about to take place. I remember that I did not respond, but I thought to myself, *I can do that.* Then, just after telling me to begin writing, He impressed me with the title of my journal. It would be: "Dying with Jesus." Immediately I began to question God why He wanted me to give it such a title. I told God, "Lawrence and I are praying for healing. We are expecting healing." Then I thought to myself:

Could God be telling me that Lawrence is not going to be healed? Just then I heard the Spirit of the Lord say to me, "This journey is not about physical death; it is about dying to self." In that moment, the Spirit shared with me that we are all dying. Every one of us is on a journey that ends in death. Death is not only a matter of our physical body, but, more importantly for those who are seeking eternal life, it is a matter of death to self. The Holy Spirit made it clear to me that the journey that my husband and I had begun was a journey of complete surrender to God. With that understanding, I reasoned that God had not promised that He was going to heal Lawrence, but neither had He indicated that He would not. I accepted the Spirit's explanation and determined that I would continue claiming healing for my husband.

Aside from my conversation with the Holy Spirit, the ride home was event free. Lawrence managed to be comfortable during the eight-hour drive home. I give thanks to our heavenly Father for that as well.

We finally reached home. It was so nice to pull into our driveway! If you could have seen our faces, you would have seen two very large smiles. We had been away from home for two months. I am sure that everyone's home is special to them. Ours, however, has a more than special place in our hearts. We tell everyone that the house we call home was a gift from God. I will say more about this later.

Once the car was parked, I walked inside with Lawrence to make sure that he made it safely to his bed. As he climbed in, I looked over and saw that he was crying. I asked him if he was all right, and he replied, "Yes, I am just so happy!" He told me that there was a moment at Loma Linda that he thought he would never see our home again. The joy he felt from walking through the doors and climbing into his own bed was just overwhelming. He was so grateful to God for yet another blessing. Again, God had shown him tremendous mercy.

As I look back on all these events, I see why God would want me to call the journey, "Dying with Jesus: *A Love Story.*" He showed us such tender love! I cannot help but pause and ask: How do we express love to our loved ones? Do we exhibit tenderness and patience. Do we spend time contemplating what we can possibly do to make their lives better? Do we seek to find ways to lessen their load? Do we put self aside in order to ensure their happiness? When they stumble or fall short of what we feel they are able, do we tenderly carry them, showing love every step of the way? A wonderfully inspired writer once wrote: "Love cannot be commanded; it cannot be won by force or authority. Only by love is love awakened" (Ellen G. White, *The Desire of Ages*, p. 22). This was Lawrence's favorite quotation, and it became mine as well. Did we struggle as most people do with this concept? Absolutely! Dying to self is something we cannot do in our own strength. It can only be accomplished in Christ. It is only when we surrender our will to Him for His guiding presence in our lives that we are able to awaken love with acts of loving kindness towards one another. This principle covers every relationship that we could ever experience—relationships with our parents, our children, our siblings, our spouse, our co-workers, our fellow church members, and our enemies. "ONLY BY LOVE IS LOVE AWAKENED." What a concept!

This is the principle that the Father uses with each of us in drawing us to Himself. In His infinite wisdom, He draws us with *blessings bestowed*. When we respond to His drawing with rebellion and selfishness, in His infinite love, He must draw us with *blessings removed*. In either case, He is showing us tremendously tender love. Our Father wants us with Him, even if it means His having to remove His blessings from us to accomplish it. God's love for us is measured by the immensity of the gift of His only begotten Son to die for our sins.

Chapter 3. *The Health Program*

While Lawrence was in the hospital, his brother Steven told us about a medical missionary who had helped a friend of his. We were able to contact the medical missionary, who agreed to fly in and stay with us for fourteen days. The plan was that he would show us the herbs and foods we needed to eat and the treatments we needed to do for my husband's cancer. He opened to us God's Word and showed us again what God's plan for man's diet has always been.

Why is it, when we buy a new appliance, car, or other major item, that we read the instruction book to properly care for it? It is because we want to get the best use of it and we want it to last as long as it can. We depend on the product manufacturer to tell us how to care for it. Yet, when it comes to our bodies, we feel that *we* know best and fail to turn to the Maker of our body to find out what He recommends we do to best care for it. God left us an instruction book; it is called the Bible. He also provided, in the writings of Ellen White, wise counsels to help us apply Bible principles of health. Lawrence and I came to believe that God knows best, and we have been vegetarians for years. Yet, there is so much more to caring for the body than not eating meat. To tell the truth, we have been convicted on several other health practices that we had refused to follow. God, in His mercy, has seen fit to allow us another opportunity to believe and obey Him. You see, we recognize that the most important thing to God is our salvation. God wants us to be with Him for eternity. He tells us, in His Word, that He winks at our ignorance. "And the times of this ignorance God winked at; but now commandeth all men every where to repent" (Acts 17:30). Once we have come into the knowledge of truth—whatever that truth is—He holds us accountable for obeying it.

Because Lawrence and I both were convicted on the truth of the health message many years ago, we knew that God would hold us accountable for not following it. We do not believe that God caused this illness to fall on Lawrence; we hold sin and Satan to blame for that. God tells us in His Word: "And we know that all things work together for good to them that love God, to them who are the called according to his purpose" (Rom. 8:28). This verse tells us that, out of mercy, God was working things out for Lawrence's welfare by allowing him another opportunity to bring his appetite under the will of God. He was giving Lawrence and me another opportunity to conform our diet to the diet that He planned for us. We recognized this to be a good and merciful thing. Ellen G. White, to whom I alluded before, is one of my favorite authors. I truly believe that all of her writings were inspired by God. Regarding appetite she wrote: "The controlling power of appetite will prove the ruin of thousands, who, if they had conquered on this point, would have had the moral power to gain the victory over every other temptation" (*Christian Temperance and Bible Hygiene*, p. 154). God's children cannot continue to allow Satan access into our life through our appetites. We must begin to control our appetites and not allow them to control us. The appetite encompasses a multitude of sins. It includes an appetite for unclean television and movies, a sinful appetite for sex, an appetite for overeating or for unhealthy foods. It includes an appetite for the things of this world in place of the spiritual food that we should be seeking from on high through the study of God's Word. Please pray with me that the Father may give us the power to surrender all of our appetites to Him. Let your prayer be: "Help us, O Lord, to refrain from all that is unclean and unhealthy for us. For we are not our own. Our bodies are your living temple." "What? know ye not that your body is the temple of the Holy Ghost which is in you, which ye have of God, and ye are not your own? For ye are bought with a price: therefore glorify God in your body, and in your spirit, which are God's" (1 Cor. 6:19, 20).

It was important to Lawrence and me that everyone know that we understood that a change of diet was not the only thing needed to take care of the cancer in his body. We fully understood that it would be God, and God alone, who would heal Lawrence—when and if He so chose. However, we also recognized our responsibility to do all that is within our ability to do, leaving the results with God. It was also important to Lawrence that you know that, while he was asking daily for God's healing hand to touch his body, it was more important to him that God save him for His kingdom. Lawrence was also praying daily that, whatever the outcome, God's will might be done and that He might be glorified.

We were now to begin the fourteen-day cleansing program. I will describe that part of our journey from my journal.

Journal Entry: *Day One*

The medical missionary arrived around 1:00 a.m. this morning. We were able to get a few hours sleep before we were to begin the program. Lawrence and I were awakened by the phone ringing at 6:00 a.m. It was my mother on the other end, urging me to turn on the television to a particular channel in order to hear the sermon that was being aired. Even though I was very tired, I got up and turned on the television. The pastor started his sermon by quoting Mark 11:24: "Therefore I say unto you, What things soever ye desire, when ye pray, believe that ye receive them, and ye shall have them." He said that we must lean on and trust in God. Then, the pastor quoted Mark 4:20: "And these are they which are sown on good ground; such as hear the word, and receive it, and bring forth fruit . . . ." The pastor explained that we must hear the word of God and receive the word of God. The child of God is to take ownership of His Word. And, finally, he quoted Ephesians 2:8: "For by grace are ye saved through faith; and that not of yourselves: it is the gift of God." He ended by saying that we are saved through grace, and we are healed through grace.

My mother had no idea that it was that morning that we were to begin our fourteen-day program with the medical missionary. I have not been able to really speak with my mother concerning my fears about my husband's illness. It is for this reason that I have no doubt that it was God who impressed my mother to call me that morning. I know that it was by divine appointment that that sermon was preached that morning. That morning God said to me, "Whatsoever you desire, when you pray, believe that ye receive them." That morning God said to me, "Receive His Word and bring forth the fruit of belief and trust." That morning God told me: "Yes, I know that you are not worthy, but, because of my grace for you and your husband, he will be healed." My God is such a mighty God! He promises to never leave us. He has been so faithful in keeping His promises to me! On such a morning as this, He sent a special message to me. Praise God for my mother being obedient to the prompting of the Holy Spirit and calling me to turn on the television! Praise God that I listened and turned the television on instead of turning over in my bed!

That sermon prompted a conversation between Lawrence and me. Lawrence told me that he wanted to be healed. Yet, he wanted to be saved even more. He went on to say that when we say that we have faith, we are really saying that we believe God's Word. If we truly believe God's Word, then we must trust what it says. God's Word never says that every sick person will be healed. Lawrence said, "I trust God, and I believe that He loves me. He loves all of us." I love my husband; he grew to be such a wise man. Again, he repeated the words, "I trust that God loves me."

Needless to say, this conversation brought forth many tears to my eyes. "God knows that I was afraid, so why should I not admit it to you?" I told my husband that morning. "I feel that the sermon was especially for me because, whenever I make my requests known to God, I always pray for His will and not mine to be done. However, in praying for your healing, if I were honest, I would have to say that I was afraid to ask for God's will to be done. God's will might not be to heal you." Lawrence held me that morning and said, "Hold on . . . hold on. We cannot let Satan destroy our confidence in God." That morning we both decided that we would accept God's decision, whatever it might be.

The medical missionary arrived, and we began our day in worship. During worship, he explained to us that the most vital aspect of this therapy would be our connection with Christ, and he said that the one sure way to achieve this connection is through prayer. He went on to explain that we can do all that Christ has shown us to do and we must do all that we know to do. Yet, it is Christ, and Christ alone, that does the healing. After worship, we had breakfast and left to purchase all of the items that we would need to complete the program. We went to the health food store for herbs and vitamins, to the grocery store for fresh produce, and to Costco for other items. Five hours after we started, we had to stop at Wal-Mart for a few additional items. It was there that something wonderful took place.

It so happens that the medical missionary's father-in-law works at the local Wal-Mart in Chico. So, after we gathered the items that we needed there, the medical missionary decided to look up his father-in-law. I took the opportunity to go to the rest room. When I came out, I was not able to locate the medical missionary, so I decided to go to the front of the store and pay for the items in our cart. When I got in line, I noticed that he had left his iPad in the cart. I proceeded to pay for all of the items and then went out to the car. I loaded the items I had purchased into the trunk and then sat down in the front seat. After a few minutes, I thought I had better call the missionary on his cell phone and let him know that I was in the car. He told me that he would be right out.

As he approached the van, the first thing he asked me was: "Do you have my iPad?" You can only imagine the panic I experienced when I realized that I had not taken the iPad from the shopping cart. I quickly got out of the van and opened the trunk to search for the iPad. I could not find it. Having left Lawrence for five hours by himself, I had been preoccupied with getting back home to him. I hoped that I had put the iPad in the van and just did not remember doing so. We searched the van and could not find it anywhere. I ran over to the place I had left my shopping cart, and the iPad was not there either. I came back to the van, and we searched two or three times more before deciding that we would go into the store to see if someone had turned it in.

To our dismay, it had not been turned in. We returned to the van and searched again. The medical missionary decided to go inside to speak with his father-in-law. He hoped his father-in-law might be of some assistance to us. While I waited in the car, I began to cry out to God. I knew that I could find a way to replace the medical missionary's iPad, but I could never replace the information he had stored in it. My heart ached for him. While I was waiting in the car for him to return, the Holy Spirit impressed me to check the cart one more time. *Maybe*, I thought, *the iPad is hidden under the plastic flap that goes down for children to sit on. The iPad is so thin—it could be there.* I got out of the van and walked over to the cart again. I lifted up the flap on the cart and, to my dismay, the iPad was not there. I turned and began walking towards my car, when a strong impression to begin praying stopped me in my tracks. I had the urgent sensation to begin pleading with

Chapter 3. The Health Program

God. However, this time the prayer was specific in nature. I was impressed by the Holy Spirit, I have no doubt, to pray that God would impress the heart of the person who had found the iPad. I prayed that God would have that person return it. Because so much time had gone by, I believed that whoever had the iPad had no intention of returning it. It was only going to be by God's grace and mercy that we would get it back. It took me only seconds to reach my car after I began pleading with God. As I stood by my car, a young women came up behind me and asked, "Are you looking for an iPad?" I fought back tears as I said, "Yes." The woman told me that she had found an iPad and had placed it in her car. She took me to her car, took out the iPad, and gave it to me.

My God is an awesome God! He is still on His throne! That woman had had no intention of returning the iPad. She had found it in the cart and, instead of turning it into the lost and found inside the store, she put it in her car and then went into the store to do her shopping. Twenty or thirty minutes later—at the very time she was coming out of the store—the Holy Spirit impressed me to get out of my car. Then He impressed me to begin praying a specific prayer, not that the iPad be returned, but that God would impress the heart of the person who had found it to return it. I will never know how God showed the young woman that it was I who had lost it. However, I do know that He directed her straight to me.

I called the missionary but could not reach him on his cell phone, so I called his wife and asked her if she could call her father and ask him to tell his son-in-law that the iPad had been returned. After the missionary got into the car and we drove off, I told him what had happened. He pondered on it for a few moments and then turned to me with the words: "God allowed this to happen because He wanted to show you that you are not alone." Then he said: "God is with you and your husband." How true his statement was! For months, we had felt God's presence with us. I agree—this was another way that God was letting me know that He was in control.

Two days later, I shared this wonderful providence with my pastor, Larre Kostenko. The medical missionary spoke up and said that the Holy Spirit had just brought back to his mind that, at the very same time I began praying my specific prayer for the changing of the heart of the person with the iPad, he too was praying for God to touch the person's heart. He had begun praying inside the store. He told me that he felt that God allowed this to happen for another reason as well. My husband was very, very sick. If God did not choose to heal him, he would die from all the cancer he had inside him. God impressed upon his mind, he said, that we must begin to plead with God for Lawrence's life the same way that we pleaded for the heart of the person who had found the iPad to be changed. He believed that God was showing us that he would hear our prayers. Was this not the very same message that God had sent me that morning? "Therefore I say unto you, what things so ever ye desire, when ye pray, believe that ye receive them, and ye shall have them" (Mark 11:24). God wants to show us His love, His power, and His grace. How many times have we not asked, and, as a result, we could not and did not receive it? Twice that day, God spoke to me. Twice He showed me that I am not alone. I trust God with my life and with my husband's life. My prayer is and always will be: "Thy will be done."

JOURNAL ENTRY: *Day Three ??*

This day began like all the others. We started with our four cups lined up on the counter full of health-reviving drinks. Then we sang a few songs and began worship. After worship, we took a short walk. Lawrence was able to walk on day one and two, but he has been so weak today that the most he could do is sit outside and get some fresh air and sunlight. Both are vital for him to get, for it helps with his recovery.

Over the past few days, Lawrence has had heat therapies and hydrotherapy. He had the "privilege" of

Chapter 3. The Health Program

experiencing hot and cold treatments. This is where Lawrence had to sit in a bucket full of hot water for five minutes and then sit in a bucket

> *I am so grateful to God that He could and would provide us a time to find humor in the midst of this storm.*

of ice and water for thirty seconds. Now, you know that I love my husband, and I am with him all the way during this time. However, I must admit that I had to leave the room while he took the hot and cold therapy. I could not stop laughing. When he sat in that bucket of ice water, oh, the sounds that came out of him! I am laughing now just thinking about it. The Bible tells us that a joyful heart does a body good and that laughter is like a medicine. I can only say that the Lord gave me a large dose of medicine when Lawrence took this treatment. Lawrence and I have always been able to laugh. He tells me all the time that I laugh at my own jokes more than anybody else. I am so grateful to God that He could and would provide us a time to find humor in the midst of this storm.

> *When you have placed your life in the hands of Jesus, you can have confidence that "all things work together for the good."*

I encourage you to look for the laughter. When you have placed your life in the hands of Jesus, you can have confidence that "all things work together for the good" (Rom. 8:28). Knowing this will give you peace and comfort that no matter how things turn out; it will be for the good. We can trust God, and with trust comes peace of mind.

Because Lawrence starts all of these therapies in a weakened state, he is left completely depleted of nearly all energy when he is done. He still has to spend most of his time in bed regaining strength. Our days have been very long. We begin each day at 5:30 a.m., and we go until 6:30 p.m., after ending the day with worship at 6:00 p.m. The medical missionary has so much planned for us, but, because Lawrence is in so much pain, he is not able to complete it all.

Journal Entry: *Day Four*

Lawrence is still having a lot of pain at night. Today, coffee enemas were introduced to his program. The missionary wanted to introduce them earlier in the program, but he did not feel Lawrence was strong enough. Lawrence felt a lot of relief after the treatment. We will continue to use them to help control his pain levels as well as detoxifying his liver. It is our prayer that the coffee enema will relieve enough of his pain that he will be able to tolerate more of the treatments as well as to take the much-needed herbs.

> *Yet, I am comforted in knowing that NOTHING comes into our lives without going through Christ.*

I cannot help thinking that, at face value, what has happened to my husband is a terrible thing. Yet, I am comforted in knowing that NOTHING comes into our lives without going through Christ. (See *Thoughts from the Mount of Blessing*, p. 71.) While He never causes the terrible things, He does allow them. Lawrence and I know that, not only did God feel that he—and we—could handle this, but God also knew that through this we would have another opportunity to become stronger and draw closer to Him. Praise God because that is what is happening!

I stated before that Lawrence's desire is for God to be glorified in this. I cannot help but stop at this point and reflect on how that prayer is being answered. There is no way that Lawrence and I could go through this except it be for God's mercy in opening our eyes that we might see His mighty hand moving on our behalf. Because our eyes have been opened we are able to share with you how much our Saviour loves us and how tenderly He walks with us in our times of need. Through this revelation of His precious love, He is glorified.

Chapter 3. The Health Program

Journal Entry: *Day Five*

We started this day with an anointing. Several of the elders of our church along with our pastor came over at 5:30 a.m. to anoint Lawrence. It was a beautiful and much-needed ceremony. We had a wonderful testimony to give. As you know, Lawrence has been very weak and in pain. His pain becomes worse as night approaches. The pain is so bad that he is unable to sleep at night. Last night he was able to sleep with little to no pain. It has been over two months that he has experienced that type of rest. All praises to God! We both were so thankful. We shared this testimony with the elders and our pastor. Our medical missionary rejoiced with us in praises to God.

Lawrence felt good and looked good. We were able to go out and walk today. He tolerated his treatments very well. He was still weak and needing to rest, but, overall, we had a very good day.

Journal Entry: *Day Seven*

We have not seen any improvement in Lawrence's condition since day five. Day five was a good day, and I continue to praise God for it. However, when Lawrence woke up on day six, the improvement he had experienced was gone. Again, he was too weak to complete most of his treatments. As night approaches, he continues to experience extreme pain. This night was worse than the others. It appears that the pain is becoming unbearable. In the late hours of the night, Lawrence had to get out of bed and go into the living room because the pain was so severe. He was unable to find a comfortable spot in the bed. On other nights, he has been able to sit in the chair next to our bed and find some relief, but, tonight, he found none. As Lawrence left the room, he told me that he was going into the living room. He had hoped that he would find comfort in his recliner. Unfortunately, comfort was not to be found.

I got up, followed my husband into the living room and made myself a place on the couch next to his chair to rest, and he began crying out for God's mercy that he would receive some peace. It seemed as if the more he prayed and cried out to God, the more intense the pain became. I had already been praying silently for God to take this pain away from my husband, and yet we saw no reprieve from the pain. However, the name of "Job" kept coming to my mind. As I thought on the story of Job, I could not help but wonder if God was telling me that Lawrence was going through a Job-like experience. The Spirit had already told me that this journey was about complete surrender to God, about dying to self. As my husband continued to cry out, I was afraid that his brother Willie would hear him and come up to investigate. I knew Lawrence would not want this; he is such a private person.

> *The Spirit had already told me that this journey was about complete surrender to God, about dying to self.*

As the pain seemed to increase and Lawrence could bear no more, his cries of pleading with God turned into praise to God. He began to repeat the words: "I trust you God.... I trust you God." Within moments of his repeating these words, the pain began to subside. Again and again he repeated, "I trust you.... I trust you," and the pain was gone. Lawrence felt good enough to get back into bed.

> *His cries of pleading with God turned into praise to God. He began to repeat the words: "I trust you God.... I trust you God."*

Lawrence and I did not talk about what had happened that night. By this time, we could not talk about much because he was so weak. It took all of his energy just to make it through the day. Yet, God spoke with me and walked with me all during the day and night. He was my comfort. I witnessed His healing hand. I know that it was the Son of God who came to my husband that night. I remembered the Spirit speaking to me on the ride home from Loma Linda, telling me that this journey has nothing to do with physical death. I remembered how the Spirit kept repeating the word "Job" in my mind, as I pleaded with Him to take this pain from my husband. I realized that I had been privileged to witness Lawrence surrendering completely to God's will. Am I saying that Lawrence felt that God had caused or sent the pain he was experiencing? I am not. I know that my husband was clear that this was caused because of sin. It could have been because of his own sins in not obeying the health laws that God had revealed to us. It could have been caused just because we live in a world of sin. It is Satan's goal to cause us pain and suffering in the hopes that we will forsake our Savior. Whatever the reason for this illness, I was witnessing my husband walking through his own Job-like experience, and, in the face of this terrible thing and this terrible pain, I witnessed him surrendering it all to God. Instead of murmuring against God, as Satan had hoped, my husband cried out for mercy, and, when it did not come, he cried out in praise: "I trust you, God. . . . I trust you." My life will never be the same after witnessing this.

Each of our days is a carbon copy of the day before. We start at 5:30 a.m. and end at 6:30 p.m. After the missionary leaves and Lawrence is resting in bed, I routinely clean up the kitchen and get things ready for the next day. Last night, as I worked in the kitchen, I could not help but reflect on what happened the night before. It was made clear to me, as I talked with God, that what Lawrence was going through at this time mirrored Job's experience. I am not saying that God had a conversation with Satan as He did in Job's case (Job 1:6–12). I have no way of knowing if that is what was happening, but I do know that Lawrence was in the process of dying to self. I was impressed to go in to talk with Lawrence. I needed to thank him for going through what he was going through.

  I walked into the bathroom, and Lawrence had pulled a chair up to the counter and was shaving. I looked at him and said, "Thank you." He looked at me with a questioning look, and yet he said nothing. I told him that God, in His wisdom, knew that, of the two of us, he was the one who would be able to handle this illness, which could be unto death. I told him that, because of how he was handling this, my faith had been strengthened. You see, during this time, we had both resolved to bring our diet under the control of the Father and to practice what we had been convicted of years prior—eating healthier. We had already given up meat, but now we were resolved to eliminate sugar and cheese from our diets. (See *The Ministry of Healing*, pp. 301, 302.) I have always struggled with sugar; we had both struggled previously with television and had stopped watching it. We spent our time, instead, in prayer. I told my husband that my life would forever be changed because of what I was witnessing in him.

Willie, Lawrence's brother, had shared with him that he had been praying for God to help him receive help with his health. He was facing so many different medical problems. Through Lawrence's illness, God had brought the medical missionary to our home. As a result, Willie was getting the help that he had prayed for. I told Lawrence that I was so sorry that he had to go through this. I knew how painful and difficult it must be. I would never have wanted this for him; however, I told him that I needed to thank him for being willing to endure this in order that God might be glorified.

JOURNAL ENTRY: *Day Twelve*

I am feeling somewhat helpless today. My husband is suffering so much. I do not know what to do.

Have you ever felt that praying just was not enough? Today I find myself asking the Lord to show me what to do. I am asking Him, "What is it you want of me right now?"

> *Have you ever felt that praying was not enough?*

God has shown Lawrence and me that He is with us. I just do not understand the delay. Each morning I wake up expecting my husband to jump out of bed, forgetting that he had been sick. Upon realizing he had been healed, we would cry and fall on our knees to give God the glory. And yet, day after day, we see no change in His condition. He continues to grow weaker and weaker.

> *I just do not understand the delay.*

Today my husband was attempting to receive his fomentation treatment, and, after five minutes, he was in so much pain that he had to lay down. He could barely make it to the room before he broke down in tears. I placed my hands on him and prayed, pleading with the Father to touch his body: "Please, God, give him peace. Give him relief."

God heard my prayer. A few moments passed, and his body began to calm down. After about twenty minutes, he felt strong enough to continue on with his treatment. So many times in life we find ourselves asking, "Is prayer enough?" I would say, "Yes, it is." Prayer is exactly what God wants of us. He wants us to see and feel our helplessness. He wants us to know that He is the one who supplies our needs. We need only ask, and yet, in asking, we must trust in Him completely. Sometimes His answer may be "no," and we must be able to accept His answer. I praise God and am so grateful that He chose to answer my prayer with a "yes" today.

JOURNAL ENTRY: *Day Thirteen*

It is the close of day thirteen. I was in the kitchen washing the dishes from our last meal of the day when my husband called me into the bedroom. He began to tell me a story that he had just heard on the television. Someone had just called in with a praise report.

The person said that he and his family were out on the sea in a boat when the sea and the waves began tossing the boat about. As the man struggled to keep control of his boat, he began to hear a voice insisting, "Command the sea to be still." He thought that it was just his fear getting the best of him. He ignored the voice and continued to struggle with the sea. Thirty minutes passed, and things did not get any better. Again, he heard a voice say, "Command the sea to be still." This time he chose to listen to the voice as that of the Holy Spirit. He stood up and commanded the sea to be still. The waves ceased to roar, and the sea became calm. The man went on to say that later he found out that fifteen of his friends were impressed to begin praying for him at the same time. This is the same type of thing that happened to me on day one of this fourteen-day journey, when I received a strong impression to pray a specific prayer for the medical missionary's missing iPad. My husband looked at me with tears in his eyes and said, "A few days ago I had a conversation with the medical missionary regarding our *commanding* God to do things. Is God telling me that we can command things of Him?" The Holy Spirit brought to my mind what had happened on day twelve, when, in my desperation, I laid hands on my husband, pleading with God to remove my husband's pain, and I reminded God that He was able to do this thing. I told Him that He had been faithful to me in the past and had answered so many of my prayers: "Because you have done this in the past, I am claiming this thing for my husband now." Some might say that I was commanding God; but I was not. I was doing as He had asked me to do—claiming blessings from the past. "When we are humble and contrite we stand where God can and will manifest Himself to us. He is well pleased when we urge past mercies and blessings as a reason why He should bestow on us greater blessings" (Ellen G. White, *Help In Daily Living*, p. 61). Lawrence thought about what I had said for a few moments, and then he said

> *"When we are humble and contrite we stand where God can and will manifest Himself to us."*

to me, "I asked God to not let me suffer, and yet it appears that it is His will that I suffer." He climbed into bed and asked me to rub his back using ointment that my daughter Trisha had brought over to help relieve his pain.

Presumption or Desire

As I began to rub his back, I felt impressed to begin praying. I began pleading with God to heal my husband. As I prayed, my mind began filling with thoughts of everything that had been taking place and of the Holy Spirit's showing us His mercies from the very beginning of this journey. As I stood there praying over my husband, the Spirit showed me that we were afraid to truly claim healing. It was there, waiting for us, and we need only claim it. I began to claim my husband's healing. I begged for the healing. I asked God to remove the pain from Lawrence and heal him. "Father," I said, "I have faith for my husband. I know you want to do this." Praise God for the Holy Spirit! I understand from God's Word that it is the Holy Spirit that tells us what to pray. The words began to flood my mind. Just like the voice that the man had heard on the boat that day, the voice told me what to say. After a season of prayer, I began to feel the assurance that my husband had been healed. God had been and will continue to be glorified through this wonderful and mighty work.

I could not stop praising God's holy name after I finished praying. The words of the old hymn, "What a Friend We Have in Jesus," began to fill my mind: "Oh, what needless pain we bear—all because we do not carry everything to God in prayer." We should not be afraid to lay our petitions at the Savior's feet. The Holy Spirit brought to my mind that there are so many wonderful things the Father wants to do for His people, but He cannot do them because we do not ask Him.

We can miss His healing if we do not ask for it. In the sermon we heard on the very first day of the health program, the pastor gave us the scripture, "Therefore I say unto you, what things so ever ye desire, when ye pray, believe that ye receive them, and ye shall have them" (Mark 11:24). Praise God! He is so good to His people! He is so faithful to us! I love Him with all my heart! My prayer is that I never sin against God again; He has healed my husband.

My husband lay resting in bed for about two hours. I decided I would take this opportunity to take my shower, all the while praising God for the great healing He had done. After my shower, I decided to spend some time at my computer writing out what had just taken place. Lawrence woke up while I was typing at my computer, and I asked if he were in pain. He said that he was not. I continued to type. After a short while, he woke up again and appeared to be having some discomfort. Disappointment began to set in. Did I misinterpret what I had just experienced? I truly believed that God had healed Lawrence, and yet he is still experiencing pain. I know that I will not be sleeping tonight; I will plead with the Father all night for my husband's healing.

Because we saw no improvement in Lawrence, I spent many hours wondering the following day. I felt so confident that the Holy Spirit was moving on my husband's behalf last night, and yet, as the hours passed, the pain returned. I asked myself: Did I miss something? In my desperation for Lawrence's healing, could I have misinterpreted the presence of the Holy Spirit? Or was the Spirit truly there and guiding my words.

Many, many weeks have passed since that night. Each time I have re-read this section of my journal, I have felt confusion about what took place that night. I truly believed that my husband had been healed, and yet he was not. My first response has been to delete the section, and yet each time I am impressed that I cannot. This was an experience that I had, and, in spite of the embarrassment I feel when talking about this, I must leave it in. Each time I have intended to delete this section, it comes to mind that, because it happened and I wrote it down, it must be important for me to keep in the journal. I have asked God what it is that needs to be shared about this particular emotion and experience that I had. The same thing happened again tonight. Once again, I came to this section and was at a loss to understand what truly took place that night. However, tonight, after working on the journal while laying in my bed, thoughts began to flood my mind. Understanding has finally come to me about that night.

Chapter 3. The Health Program

I have come to understand that we humans can want something so badly that we misunderstand the signs. God does not err, nor can He lie. I wanted healing so badly for my husband that I misunderstood the feelings of peace and assurance that came over me as I prayed that night.

God's Spirit draws close to us when we pray to Him. When this happens, we cannot help but feel His presence and the peace and comfort that come with it. Lawrence expressed it on day one of the cleansing program: "God never promised to heal everyone." That is true, yet God did promise to draw close to us in times of trials and suffering. What happened is that I wanted so much for my husband to be healed that I took a leap that night and assumed that the peace and comfort I received from pouring out my heart to the Father was His assurance that my husband had been healed.

God understands our human emotions oh so well; He created them. His presence did bring comfort to Lawrence that night. His pain did leave him for several hours, and, when it returned, it was not as severe. He was able to sleep, though he was not healed. I was very disappointed when I realized that Lawrence had not been healed that night, yet I knew by faith that I had to continue to hold onto the hand of Jesus, even though I did not understand at the time how I could have been so mistaken.

We must know that, when there is an error, the error is not with God or His Word. We must trust in His love for us and continue to seek His face (Psalm 105:4). We must pray that our eyes will be opened and our error be made clear to us. Christ says, "Seek, and ye shall find; knock, and it shall be opened unto you" (Matt. 7:7). Lawrence and I were both praying that he might be healed, but, more than that, Lawrence was asking that he be saved. That night, God began to give me the assurance that Lawrence would be raised from his bed of affliction; however, I did not know if God would raise him now or at the first resurrection.

Journal Entry: *Day Fourteen*

Our fourteen days with the medical missionary will end today. We have seen very little improvement in Lawrence's condition. He has been too sick to do the program that was prepared for him, but we knew and understood that it would not be the program that healed Lawrence. Rather, it would be God, and God alone, who did the healing.

We could never express fully what it has meant to us to receive the spiritual guidance that we received from the missionary. However things turn out with Lawrence, our family will forever be grateful for the sacrifice that he and his family made in allowing him to be apart from them to be with us. The knowledge that we have received regarding God's plan for us in diet will be with us until we die. We have a newfound commitment to follow God's plan. We will continue to pray that God will help us to surrender daily to this plan, deny self, take up our cross, and follow Him.

Chapter 4. *Gethsemane*

The medical missionary has been gone for a few days now, and Lawrence still has not been able to complete the program that was laid out for him. Nonetheless, we try each day to do what we can. I have read in the Bible that the dragon is angry with the remnant of God's seed and went to make war with God's people (Rev. 12). The Scriptures tell us that, in the last days, we are going to have a time of trouble like never before. I must encourage you to study the book of Revelation. Many are under the impression that we cannot understand this book. However, Jesus says in that very book, "If any man have an ear, let him hear" (Rev. 13:9).

Would a loving God full of mercy for His people leave us in darkness? Absolutely not! God's Word is clear, and, with the help of the Holy Spirit, we can understand what God has revealed to us in Revelation about the time just before Christ's return.

The Bible tells us that God is going to have a people here at that time who will be true to His teachings. God declares in Revelation: "Here is the patience of the saints: here are they that keep the commandments of God, and the faith of Jesus Christ" (Rev. 14:12). In the Scriptures we are told that, during this time, there will be people out to do the work of Satan and destroy God's remnant. We will not be able to buy or sell; the Holy Spirit will have been withdrawn from the face of the earth for those who have rejected Him; those that will stand will need to have a faith that is unmovable. Please, please, do not let this time come upon you by surprise. There is a wonderful little book by Ellen White, adapted from *The Great Controversy*, entitled *The Great Hope*. It will help you understand that God, in His mercy, is trying to prepare us for this time. The trials and difficulties we go through are to strengthen us and build our faith. Each time that we go to the Father and He delivers us, our faith should be strengthened. These occurrences in our lives can be called our own little time of trouble. During these times, we will undergo the "Gethsemane experience." Some might ask, "What is the 'Gethsemane experience'?" It is the experience that Christ went through just before He was crucified. Even before His betrayal, Christ knew that His time had come. The cross was just before Him. As Jesus and His disciples arrived at the olive grove known as Gethsemane, He commanded three of His disciples: "Tarry ye here, and watch with me" (Matt. 26:38). He went a short distance from them and then experienced such emotional pain that He sweat great drops of blood.

> *The trials and difficulties we go through are to strengthen us and build our faith. Each time that He delivers us, our faith should be strengthened.*

I was blessed to be a witness to Lawrence's "Gethsemane experience" last night. Lawrence has been suffering so much with the pain from the cancer taking over his body. As the sun sets each evening, the pain begins to increase. We have prayed for God's healing hand to touch him, and I believe that God has showed us in so many ways that He is right here with us. However, we do not have the complete assurance that it is God's will for Lawrence to be healed, for he continues to suffer. My husband called me into the room tonight and explained to me that he had just prayed that the Lord would take him in his sleep that very night if it is not possible for him to be healed.

> *My husband explained to me that he had just prayed that the Lord would take him in his sleep that very night.*

I stood speechless for a few moments and then responded: "I am not sure how to process what you have just told me." You see, I love my husband very much, and I want him here with me. Yet, I watch him suffering in pain night after night, pleading for God's mercy to relieve him of the pain that fills his body. Some nights the hand of mercy touches his body and the pain subsides. Other nights he gets but a few moments of sleep. Naturally, I do not want him to continue suffering. I believe that it would be selfish on my part to pray contrary to what he is praying. Lawrence went on to tell me that he did not want to cause me any more stress. However, he needed me to know what he had just prayed because he did not want me to be unprepared if God should grant his prayer. He also wanted me to share with his mother what he had prayed. He knew that it would be very difficult for his mother if he should pass away, yet he felt that it would make it easier for her to bear if she knew his passing was an answer to his prayer. After he shared this with me, all I could do was stop what I was doing in the kitchen, curl up next to him in bed, and ask the Lord for His will to be done.

As you might expect, the night was terrible. It was extremely emotional for me, and Lawrence suffered not only physically but emotionally as well.

As the night progressed, so did Lawrence's pain. The pain became so severe that Lawrence began to think that God was not pleased with his request. There was nothing that we could do to stop Lawrence's pain. The pain medication that I gave him did not seem to touch the pain. I found myself curled up behind him holding him in my arms, praying that he would find some relief. As I lay holding him, he began to cry out to God, "I'm sorry . . . I'm sorry for praying that prayer." Then he told me, "I believe I am having so much pain because I prayed such a selfish prayer." He told me that the greater severity of his pain led him to believe that God was punishing him for his prayer.

Every night was filled with pain for Lawrence. Yet, the greater pain that he experienced that night he connected with his prayer. I told Lawrence that that could not be possible. The God that I serve would never punish him for a prayer such as he had prayed that night. He is too loving to do that. I reminded Lawrence that

God knows his heart and his circumstances and that God would never condemn him for praying a prayer requesting mercy. Then I told Lawrence that, if there was anything missing in his prayer, that he could be comforted in knowing that the Holy Spirit had made it right for him before it reached the Father, for the Bible tells us that our prayers are made right by being mingled with the interceding of the Spirit before reaching our heavenly Father (Rom. 8:26). Lawrence responded in agreement with what I told him.

Some time passed, the severity of Lawrence's pain began to subside, and we were both able to fall asleep. However, I found myself waking up several times before morning. Each time I awoke, I would lie quietly looking at Lawrence to see if I could see him breathing or his body moving. I did not know if God would choose to honor Lawrence's prayer that night and take him in his sleep. I recognized that it was in God's power so to do. Finally, the morning came. I was so happy to see that Lawrence was still with me. I went into the kitchen to prepare for the morning, and, when I returned to the bedroom, I noticed that Lawrence was sitting in the chair next to our bed. He appeared to be in deep thought. I stood by for a few moments, and then he looked up at me and said, "I guess God has decided that I suffer a while longer." I wasn't quite sure how to respond to his comment, so I didn't. I told him that I was going out front to walk for a while.

> *I did not know if God would choose to honor Lawrence's prayer. I recognized that it was in God's power so to do.*

As I began to walk, I continued contemplating what had happened the night before. I heard the Holy Spirit whisper, "Gethsemane, Gethsemane." Then thoughts began rushing into my mind. There was the thought of Jesus' anticipation of the cross, pleading for mercy from His Father that the cup of suffering be taken from Him. There were the thoughts of the night that Lawrence had just past and how he had cried out for mercy: "Please let me go in my sleep, Father! Let me go tonight. If there is any way. Please let me go tonight. Please don't allow me to suffer like this any more." The Holy Spirit linked Christ's words to His Father, "Nevertheless, not my will, but thine, be done," with

Chapter 4. Gethsemane

Lawrence's prayer, "If there is no possibility that I will be healed, let me go." Then, the words Lawrence had spoken to me on day one of the program rang out in my head: "I trust God, and I believe that He loves me." Lawrence's prayer has always been for God's will to be done and that he stay faithful to God.

> *I heard the Holy Spirit whisper, "Gethsemane, Gethsemane." Thoughts began rushing into my mind.*

As I walked, the Holy Spirit was showing me that the prayer that Christ prayed in Gethsemane and the prayer Lawrence had prayed were linked together. When I finished my morning walk, I came inside, and Lawrence and I both remained in deep thought over the events of the night. As the morning went on, neither of us spoke about what had taken place the night before. I realized that Lawrence must be processing the prayer that he had made and the answer that the Lord was apparently giving. Later that morning as we sat at the table eating our breakfast, there wasn't much conversation. It wasn't until I was in the kitchen cleaning up after our meal that I found that I could no longer keep silent. I walked over to my husband, and I said, "I am so sorry that you are suffering so much. I don't want you to be in pain. It has been months that you have gone through this, but I have to tell you that I was so happy when I woke up this morning and you were still with me." Lawrence didn't respond; he just looked up and smiled at me. I could tell that Lawrence was still in deep thought, trying to understand what had happened the night before.

Later that day, I walked into the room, and Lawrence was sitting once again in the chair next to the bed in deep thought. He looked up at me and said, "I have asked God to forgive me for praying that prayer last night. I have asked God to forgive me for my lack of faith in praying such a prayer." As Lawrence spoke, the Holy Spirit again repeated the word "Gethsemane." Twice I heard the word "Gethsemane, Gethsemane." With that prompting, I began to share with Lawrence what God had been showing me throughout that day as I pondered the events of the previous night. I said, "Honey, all day today, whenever I would think about what happened last night, the word 'Gethsemane' came to mind."

I shared with him how the Holy Spirit had reminded me of how Christ, just before His crucifixion, prayed that the Father would take the cup from Him. I explained to him that I believed that God wanted him to know that there is no sin in praying such a prayer. Then I reminded him how much agony Christ felt that night in Gethsemane. Christ returned to find the disciples sleeping after He had asked them to watch and pray with Him, as Ellen White aptly describes:

> The Son of God was seized with superhuman agony, and fainting and exhausted, He staggered back to the place of His former struggle. His suffering was even greater than before. As the agony of soul came upon Him, "His sweat was as it were great drops of blood falling down to the ground." The cypress and palm trees were the silent witnesses of His anguish. (*The Desire of Ages*, p. 689)

Lawrence listened quietly as I shared with him what the Lord had been bringing to my mind all day, as I thought about what had happened the night before and the similarities between his prayer and Christ's prayer in Gethsemane. He began to realize that God understood his cries for mercy. As Lawrence and I spoke, I began to see a sense of resolve come over my husband. It is hard to explain it, but I saw his countenance change that day. He had asked God to remove this cup from him, and God's answer was, "Not yet." Lawrence accepted God's answer in the matter and found peace. From that day on, there was a peace on my husband's countenance that I had not seen before. It was a peace that could only have come from his complete surrender to God's will. After that night, Lawrence did not suffer with pain as he had so many nights before. Whatever pain he endured he did so with a peace and confidence that is hard for me to explain. I believe Lawrence had completely surrendered his will to God's control.

> *He began to realize that God understood his cries for mercy. God's answer was, "Not yet." Lawrence accepted God's answer and found peace.*

CHAPTER 4. GETHSEMANE

This has brought back to my mind the question I had for God when He first gave me the title to use for this journey, "Dying with Jesus." At that time, I told Him, "Father, we are expecting healing. Why would you have me title this 'Dying with Jesus'?" He told me through His Spirit that this was not just about physical death. It was about dying to self.

I truly believe that Lawrence was fighting his last battle with self as he cried out in agony and as I lay with my arms wrapped around him trying to comfort and reassure him that God would never punish him for having prayed a prayer to have his bitter cup removed.

The following days, I spent a lot of time in thought, trying to process his prayer request and remembering that, instead of his pain subsiding, it had become more intense. Lawrence shared with me that the pain he felt after he had prayed for God to allow him to die in his sleep that night was far more severe than any pain he had felt before. The Holy Spirit brought to my mind the story of Jacob and Esau, and the Spirit flashed before my mind the struggle Jacob had with Christ (Genesis 32). The Spirit also brought to my mind the time that Christ came for Moses, and Satan tried to keep Him from taking Moses' body (Jude 9). Satan was claiming Moses as his own. The story of Job came again to my mind (Job 1). The Lord had been showing me the story of Job for some time.

I must say again that God, in His infinite mercy, knew that Lawrence, like Job, would be able to withstand this attack of Satan. God knew that Lawrence still battled, as we all do, with self on some level. However, knowing all things, God also knew that, when faced with the direst of circumstances, Lawrence would lean on Christ to see Him through. That is what Lawrence was doing!

I believe that Satan knew he had one last chance to get Lawrence to curse God and turn away from His loving arms. Satan tormented my husband so severely the previous night. For hours, Lawrence kept asking me why the pain was so bad when it had never been this bad before—and he had had

> *I believe that Satan knew he had one last chance to get Lawrence to curse God and turn away from His loving arms.*

some very bad nights. I lay watching my husband as he held onto the hand of Jesus that night. It was as if Lawrence were saying, "I won't let go until you bless me." I truly believe I witnessed that night the final battle for my husband's soul, and Satan lost while our God was victorious! Our God is able to carry us through, as Hebrews says: "Wherefore he is able also to save them to the uttermost that come unto God by him, seeing he ever liveth to make intercession for them" (Heb. 7:25).

It is so important that we build a trusting relationship with the Father. We should know that, in spite of our circumstances, God is in control and that He will exercise all power to save and deliver us out of the hand of Satan. We cannot focus our attention on the things that Satan throws our way. We must look to Christ our deliverer to see us through. We must trust Him to show us what it is that He would have us to do. As you face life's challenges, trust in God. Trust in the Lord of the universe to see you through life's most difficult times. His divine heart cries out in pain when we hurt. Such suffering is not what He planned for us when He created this world. "Hold on; hold on," He calls. We have but a little longer to be here, and there is much work to do for our Saviour! Christ declares: "I must work the works of him that sent me, while it is day: the night cometh, when no man can work" (John 9:4). We do not know when our time on this earth will end. However, we can rest assured that, when that time comes, Satan will try to claim us as his own. If you have surrendered your will to the will of the Father, Christ will hold up His hands and say, "My blood is sufficient for you!"

> *It is so important that we build a trusting relationship with God.*

Chapter 5. *It's Personal*

The faith in God that I was privileged to witness in my husband was a faith that had been nurtured and strengthened through years of trusting God. There were many things in Lawrence's life that he was ashamed of. There were many things for which he has asked God to forgive him. Back in 2004, Lawrence and I were attending an afternoon Bible study, during which someone spoke about a sin to which Lawrence and I had both succumbed. I remember thinking about it at the time it was mentioned, but I asked God to forgive me, and I accepted His forgiveness. Without my knowing, however, the same comment had struck a cord in my husband's heart. It was not until almost two weeks later, when I walked into the living room and found him sobbing, that I found out how that comment had effected him.

> *The faith in God that I was privileged to witness in my husband was a faith that had been nurtured and strengthened through years of trusting God.*

There he was crying. When I inquired what was wrong, he began to tell me what had been taking place for close to two weeks. He began telling me that, on that particular Sabbath almost two weeks before, he heard a comment that caused him to question whether God had really forgiven him. He told me that he has loved God all of his life and that he believed in God but that he had never experienced God on a personal level. He said that he had begun asking God for confirmation that he had, without a doubt, been forgiven. He told me that he had decided to keep his feeling about this to himself. He did not want to talk to anyone except God. He wanted God, and God alone, to speak to him. Several days passed, and he did not receive peace. This troubled him greatly. He needed to know that he had been forgiven. After a few more days passed, he said that he received a strong impression to get and open a letter that had come in the mail. In Southern California, we have a friend named Gail who has a ministry of sending out a monthly index card with specific scriptures on it. When Lawrence and I moved to Oroville, Gail began sending cards and scriptures to us here. Apparently, we had gotten one in the mail, which Lawrence had not stopped to open when it arrived. He told me that he had ignored the prompting of the Holy Spirit to get the letter and open it. For several more days, he continued to anguish over whether or not he had truly been forgiven. We were approaching another Sabbath, and peace had not come to him. As he sat in the living room talking to God, he received another very strong impression to go get the letter and open it. This time, Lawrence decided to obey the prompting, and he got up and found the letter. As usual, it contained a card with scriptures for us. One by one, he began looking up the scriptures, and this is what he found:

> *He wanted God, and God alone, to speak to him.*

> Brethren, I count not myself to have apprehended: but this one thing I do, forgetting those things which are behind, and reaching forth unto those things which are before, I press toward the mark for the prize of the high calling of God in Christ Jesus. (Phil. 3:13, 14)

> But he was wounded for our transgressions, he was bruised for our iniquities: the chastisement of our peace was upon him; and with his stripes we are healed. (Isa. 53:5)

Trust in the Lord with all thine heart; and lean not unto thine own understanding. In all thy ways acknowledge him, and he shall direct thy paths. (Prov. 3:5, 6)

God showed complete mercy and love to Lawrence that day. God tells us that, before we call, He will answer: "And it shall come to pass, that before they call, I will answer; and while they are yet speaking, I will hear" (Isa. 65:24). Lawrence ignored the promptings of the Holy Spirit. As a result, he anguished for several days more than he would have done if he had followed the Spirit's promptings immediately, even though he did not fully understand why he was being told to get the letter.

Our dear friend, Gail, had no way of knowing that Lawrence would need these very texts to show him that God had forgiven him. Yet, in her faithfulness to the prompting of the Holy Spirit, she sent the very text that would speak to Lawrence and show him that he was truly forgiven. We received this letter a few weeks before the Bible study, at which Lawrence was convicted, had even taken place. The letter was sitting on the counter, waiting for the very moment that Lawrence would need to read it. Lawrence's anguish had to do with whether God had accepted his repentance. He knew that many people had been hurt by his actions. Pain and suffering were a direct effect of our actions, and, many years later, we still saw the results of the pain that we had caused. Lawrence needed to know, without a doubt, that God had forgiven him and that his path was now directed by his Saviour. As he read the verses, God spoke to him through His Word. He told Lawrence to "forget the things which are behind him" and to "press toward the mark for the high calling of God in Christ." Satan is the "accuser of our brethren" (Rev. 12:10). It is through his attempts to keep before us our sins that he hopes to make us feel defeated. Christ directs us to forget those things and press toward the mark of God's high calling. Christ also told Lawrence that day that He had been wounded for his transgressions . . . yet with His stripes Lawrence would be healed. Christ encouraged him to trust in Him with all his heart and to lean not on his own understanding. Continue to acknowledge me, Christ had said, and I will direct your paths.

It was by divine appointment that these very texts came to Lawrence in anticipation of the very time that he needed to hear God's voice. Lawrence was not the same after that day. He knew that God was real and that God had heard his cries. He knew that God had forgiven him, and, though he had caused so much pain to others, God, in His infinite mercy, would work all things together for good (Rom. 8:28). Lawrence told me that He knew God was real before this, however, he had never experienced him personally. He remembered thinking several times throughout his years, as others shared their testimony, that he had not experienced God in a personal way. Lawrence's relationship with God moved from abstract to intimate. He knew that God had answered his cries. Satan placed doubt in Lawrence's mind, but Christ replaced the doubt with the assurance of forgiveness. Lawrence's walk with God was not the same after that.

I have said it before, and I will say it again: we serve a God who is all knowing. Despite the way things appear, God is in control. We can trust Him to be with us and to never abandon us. Lawrence shared this testimony with others on several occasions, and each time he could not help but come to tears as he thought about how much God loved him. This revelation of God's love and mercy took place in 2004. The card that he received in the mail that month and read under the Spirit's promptings remains in his Bible to this day as a constant reminder of God's forgiveness and tender mercies.

The reason that God asked me to title this journey, "Dying with Jesus: A Love Story," is because it describes what our lives can and should be—a constant unfolding of God's true love for each of us.

Journal Entry: *"The Journey Continues"*

There is no real change in my husband's condition today. Each morning, part of our program is to walk an hour. Because Lawrence is too weak to walk, he sits on the front porch and gets fresh air and sunlight while I walk for about thirty minutes out front. This is a morning of praise and thanksgiving to the God of heaven. He is so faithful to us as we continue on day after day!

Even though I see no change in Lawrence, and I don't understand why he has delayed healing him, I trust that God has a plan. I will wait to see His plan revealed. Lawrence and I pray daily that God will be glorified, and we trust that He is working things out to that end. Last night, I spoke with our dear friend Pastor Warren Muir. He stopped by to visit with Lawrence, yet Lawrence was unable to accept company. It takes too much energy for him to talk right now. During Pastor Muir's visit, I shared with him that God has revealed to me that it is His plan that Lawrence be raised from this bed of illness. However, I told him that I did not have the complete assurance whether it would be now or at the first resurrection. Therefore, I wait, trusting in God's divine wisdom.

JOURNAL ENTRY: *"Moment of Despair"*

Today my husband is very, very weak. Each day we continue to hold onto the hope that he will be healed, and yet we see no change in him. Lawrence has had such a peace about him. Yet, today Lawrence appears to be weary, and it wearies me to see him so tired of the struggle. I can see that he is fighting feelings of hopelessness. We just need to hold on.

As I looked at my husband's face this evening, I could see he is in deep thought. His spirits appear very low. He is very tired and fatigued from the days of no energy and not feeling well. I stood at the foot of the bed looking at him, not knowing what I could say to lift his spirits. Just then the Holy Spirit brought the words to my mind that Lawrence had said to me that first morning: "Hold on; we have to hold on, Brenda."

As those words flashed through my mind, God impressed my mind with a picture. In my mind, I could see Christ, reaching down from heaven. Leaning over with His arms stretched out wide and long, reaching—reaching down for us. In an instant, I saw Lawrence and me reaching up. We were trying so very hard to touch the hands of Christ. We could not reach Him, nor He us, but we kept reaching up as Christ kept reaching down. Finally, our hands touched, and we clasped hands together. As we held hands, I could hear Christ saying, "Hold on, hold on." Immediately, I began to tell Lawrence what the Holy Spirit had shown me, and I said, "Honey, we must hold on. We have to just hold on!" Lawrence did not respond. At this point, he was not able to talk much. Yet, I could see the expression on his face soften and his countenance reflecting peace. This was one of the many nights that everything stopped. I laid aside the things that needed to be done concerning the house and simply climbed into bed with Lawrence for the night. Whatever else needed to be done would have to wait until the next day. For years, Lawrence and I would say to each other that, as long as we were able to end our days in bed together, with him curled up behind me or me curled up behind him, all was right in the world. So, that is what I would do when things seemed heavy for him. I stopped everything and curled up next to him. For that moment, all was right in our world.

    I cannot help but think how that, from the beginning, God has been showing Lawrence and me that He is with us. He did not leave us to go through this trial alone. We are unworthy of his precious gift—unworthy to receive the love that He has chosen to bestow upon us. I know that Christ does not bless us because we deserve it. He blesses us because He loves us. "But God commendeth his love toward us, in that, while we were yet sinners, Christ died for us" (Rom. 5:8). The song writer said it so eloquently when he wrote: "Oh, how I love Jesus! Oh, how I love Jesus! Oh, how I love Jesus because He first loved me." The scripture comes to mind: "What is man, that thou art mindful of him? and the son of man, that thou visitest him?" (Psalm 8:4). I stood beside my husband, not knowing what words would bring peace to his heart, and, in an instant, Christ told me what to say. What love! What tender love! Thank you, Jesus! Thank you!

Chapter 5. It's Personal

Journal Entry: *"God Provides"*

I have shared with you the blessing of how the journey to Loma Linda began and how the God of heaven provided for our needs. I have shared how He started providing for us months before we even knew that there would be a need. I have shared the circumstances that provided us with the money that was needed to make such a trip possible. Step by step, God has been providing and showing us the way—showing us that He is here with us.

The journey continues, and we do not see improvement in Lawrence's condition. He will have a couple of good days and then it is as if we are starting all over again. His energy levels are completely gone, and his pain levels are high, but God continues to be with us.

As I mentioned before, Lawrence and I own a care home for the elderly. While we were away from home in Loma Linda, one major thing after another began to happen. Financial stumbling blocks began to arise. We had to increase our payroll because I was no longer available to work my usual job, so we were now having to pay someone to work my hours, increasing our payroll and insurances. Our septic pump went out twice, costing us thousands of dollars to have it replaced. Our hot water heater has been out for weeks. We have already poured money into it, and it looks as if additional parts will be needed. The expense of the medical missionary and all of the herbs that we had to purchase, along with the supplies needed for the treatments, have mostly been floated on credit cards. Yet, during all of this, we continue to say that this too is in God's hands. He has shown us His mercy; He has been our ever-present help. We choose not to question. We will only move forward, trusting that God will provide.

Today God has poured down upon us a large sum of money that we did not expect. Lawrence's supplemental insurance has been paying out on his claim for several months now. We thought that we only had a few small payments left. Today we received our final check from the insurance company. The check was for ten thousand dollars. Praises be to the God of the universe! He is merciful! I continue to say: Trust in the Lord, move forward, and do not worry about the circumstances that you see before you. Satan might appear to be in control of things, and he will beat us down as much as he can to discourage us in these last days. His plan is to get us caught up in discouragement and the things of this world rather than focusing on Christ and His ability to provide for our needs and to work out circumstances for our good. We cannot allow Satan to win. Our Father is still on the throne, and He will not withhold anything from us if it be for our good. "My God will supply all your need according to His riches in glory by Christ Jesus" (Phil. 4:19). Stand the test of your trials. Call on the name of Jesus. Tell Satan that he is a liar. Do not be discouraged. Everything that has happened in the last few months the Lord has provided the money to manage. God has not left one area of our life unattended. God can and will do the same for you. I am overwhelmed with His mercy, goodness, and love for each one of us. I do not know why He has chosen to bless us, but He has, and I praise His holy name! I will continue to praise His holy name forever! When despair seems to overtake me, God sends a sign like this to let me know that He is still with us.

JOURNAL ENTRY: *Sabbath Morning, September 1, 2012*

Blessed, blessed Sabbath morning. The Holy Spirit reveals His moving hand once more. I was impressed to call a friend this morning. She is a close friend; we have been friends for over thirty years. The situation with Lawrence's health has really left her discouraged and devastated. However, I just found out this morning that she has not been able to pray or listen to anything spiritual because of the anger she is feeling. She let me know that she has been asking God, "How could you allow something like this to happen to someone who I know loves you and is trying to serve you?"

She went on to say, "I sat on the side of my bed last night, Brenda, and I felt impressed that I needed to tell the Lord I am back." She said that she told God that she was sorry for leaving Him for a time but that she was back and felt impressed that she needed to find a church home for her family.

Let me interject a little background here. We recently sent out a letter to all of our family and friends, updating them on what has been going on with us and sharing how God has been with us through this whole experience. The letter, she told me, prompted her to think about her relationship with God and how she needed to trust God more. I was able to share with her how God had just shown me that He has all authority. Satan is in control of circumstances on earth, but, when Christ decides to step in with His authority, everything works out for our good. I went on to share with her how we must praise God through the good times and through the bad. "My brethren, count it all joy when ye fall into divers temptations" (James 1:2). When things are going fine, praise Him. Then pray, when things appear to be going wrong, that you will be able to praise Him for all the good times and for all the times He has delivered you in the past.

It is a miracle how God can use the act of encouraging another to your own encouragement. Somehow, when you speak the words, they seem to echo back in your ear. Sharing with her how God has authority, in spite of how things look, reminded me of a sermon I heard when we were in Loma Linda. As I have said, there we had all the vegetarian food readily accessible to us. 3ABN was provided through the cable company. We could go into the multi-purpose room, relax, and watch 3ABN. It was heaven to us. I remember saying to Lawrence: "God has shown us that He is with us in a special way. Yet, I am not sure why He has chosen to draw so close to us now." Then I said, "My prayer is that, when things turn and life appears to be its worst, I will be able to praise Him just as I am praising Him now." I thank God for bringing this back to my mind because, during this great trial, He has been very close to Lawrence and me. I love Him so much, and I still give Him praise. I don't question why this thing has happened. I am sure that there are many reasons. Do I think that God caused this illness to happen? No, I do not. It is a natural progression of our going against the health practices and laws that He has laid before us. Yet, there are people who practice the health laws and still come down with diseases. Are they being punished? No, no, no. It is not a punishment. As I told my friend Valinda, God wants us to have complete and total trust in Him. We need unquestioning faith in the Father, and we need to have an undying love for Him as well. Just as we need to exercise our arms, legs, and abdominal muscles if we want to stay in shape, we also have to exercise our faith. If we never had any trials through which we had to hold onto Jesus' hand to get through, our faith would never grow.

In God's mercy and love for us, He allows—not causes—things such as this to happen so that we will grow stronger and have more trust in His saving, providing, and nurturing power. He loves us so much, how can we help but love Him?

Inspiration tells us how important it is for us to study God's Word. We are to memorize Scripture and song. It is during times of trial and tribulation that the Holy Spirit brings these songs, words, and scriptures back to our minds and hearts to encourage and strengthen us. If we are slack in studying God's Word and learning gospel songs, the Holy Spirit has nothing to bring back to our minds. I encourage you, brother and sister, to study God's Word. I admit that I have not studied as much as I should have, but I know that Lawrence has studied hours on end. I have no doubt that, as the Lord is bringing His Word back to my mind to strengthen me, so is He encouraging and strengthening Lawrence through Scripture and song. I know that Lawrence is holding on—with every ounce of strength that he has in his body—to every word that comes out of the mouth of God. Just the other day, Lawrence asked me to find his book of promises. He said that he wanted to read them and dwell on them every day.

Chapter 6. *Nearer Still Nearer*

For some time, the Lord has been bringing to mind songs that I have learned over the years. It is never the whole song. That could be because I have never memorized all the words to these wonderful hymns in our hymnal. Yet, the Holy Spirit, in His faithfulness to me, has been bringing back phrases from these songs. The words of these songs have given me comfort. Each time this has happened, I have recognized that it was the Spirit who was bringing the words to mind because they are always appropriate for the concerns that I was feeling at the time.

On one particular day, I was pondering just how sick my husband truly was. I had been asking, "God, is your answer going to be 'yes'?" Each morning I looked for Lawrence to wake up and jump out of bed like he has done in the past, forgetting that he had been sick. I imagined that, after being up for a short while, he would realize that Christ's healing hand had touched him in the night and we would begin to praise God. Yet, day after day, we wake up and there has been no change in his condition. On that day, the words to the song, "What a Mighty God we Serve," kept coming to my mind over and over again: "What a mighty God we serve!" I know that God wanted me to be comforted in knowing that He is a mighty God who can do as He wills to do.

In thinking on the delays in Lawrence's healing, the Lord also brought to my mind the words of a sermon I recently had heard, preached by a pastor in Southern California, Pastor Michael B. Kelly, II. In his sermon series entitled, "Crucial Conversations," Pastor Kelly said that we often find ourselves in circumstances that seem out of our control because Satan has stepped in, causing things to happen. I could certainly relate to that. In our case, it is my husband's devastating illness. Pastor Kelly went on to say, "When things seem out of control and in the hands of Satan, it is then that Jesus steps in with all authority. We read in the first part of Mark 5 that Jesus has authority over the demons; in the second part of Mark 5, that He has authority over disease; in the last part of Mark 5, that He has authority over death. What Mark is trying to get us to see here is that your God—my God—has authority." Then he said, "I know, without a doubt, that it is the devil that causes problems to occur. The devil gets up in our lives and causes things to go wrong, causes things to mess up. We find ourselves crying out many times, saying, 'God what's up? I don't feel like you are in control.' God says to us, 'That's all right, because, when you don't feel like I'm in control, watch me exercise My authority.' Even though the demoniac was under the control of Satan, when Jesus exercised His authority, something happened to Satan's control." Pastor Kelly said that we should be at peace when different things in our life seem out of control because God will ultimately exercise His authority. We are to praise God daily, even though we do not know how or when God will take care of the problem. What we do know is that our God is able to work all situations out for our good (Rom. 8:28). Pastor Kelly said: "Our God may not seem like He is in control, but He has all authority. We've got to understand that there will be moments in our lives when it doesn't look like God is in control, but that does not matter because He has full authority over all situations, and when He exercises authority, whoever appears to be in control of things at the time must give up control to the one who has the authority. God says, 'So you're being controlled by a demon? I've got authority. So you've got a disease? I've got authority. You've got a bad situation? I've got authority.' Your God—my God—has authority. He can speak to your situation because He has authority. We have a God who has authority. Sometimes we need to just wait for Him to exercise His authority. The crazy part about it is that sometimes it might look like He won't exercise His authority. Maybe somebody dies. Well, He will exercise His authority all right because one day the sky is going to crack open and He is going to say, 'Come forth,' and, with all authority, death will not be able to hold that person in. Why? Because death might have been in control, but Christ has the authority." I knew that God had sent that message for me, but I did not know, at the time, all that God intended to communicate to me.

Some might say that it was just a coincidence that I visited Pastor Kelly's church in Riverside, California. Some might say that it was by chance that I stopped at the table as I left the church that afternoon and picked up a few CDs, one of which had this message on it. But those of you who know God as I do, know that there are no mere coincidences in the life of a Christian. I have given my life to Christ; I trust Him completely. He is guiding my path every day. He knew what was ahead of me, and He placed that sermon in my hands for the sole purpose of using those words to comfort me today. Do you see why I continue to declare that Christ loves us so much? How much time and planning went into orchestrating things for me? God knew that there would be a delay in His answering our prayers. He knew that I would be asking, "God are you going to answer 'yes'?" In His loving mercy, He set me up to hear this message to encourage me and strengthen my faith. After giving me this sermon, He brought the words back to my mind when I needed them most. I have no doubt that the words of this sermon were given as a special message for me. What a mighty God we serve! What a loving God we serve! My prayer is for God to keep my eyes open that I may see His wondrous love for me. Please know that I am also praying that God will open each of your eyes that you may also see how He is working on your behalf. He loves you so much!

JOURNAL ENTRY: *"Reflecting on Past Blessings"*

"He is well pleased when we urge past mercies and blessings as a reason why He should bestow on us higher and greater blessings" (Ellen G. White, *Help in Daily Living*, p. 61).

A few days have passed. I am feeling very sad this morning. As part of the program each morning after devotion, I walk for thirty minutes. Today the tears flow from my eyes as I try to record the recent events of this journey. I continue to see my husband growing weaker and weaker. This morning the Holy Spirit has brought to my mind the story of Martha and Mary as their brother lay sick and dying. I can so relate to what they must have been feeling. It is very hard for me to record my thoughts this morning because of the tears that are pouring down my face. I feel it is important that I share with you what the Holy Spirit has shared with me this morning in spite of the pain that I am feeling. It comes to mind how I have read that the word went out to Christ: "Lazarus is sick unto death. Please come." Then days passed, and Christ did not come. Martha and Mary watched as Lazarus was slowly slipping away. That is how I am feeling this morning. My husband is sick unto death, and I have prayed for Christ to come and touch his body, and Christ has not come. Lawrence is slowly, slowly slipping away from me. His body is so frail, and he has lost so much weight. When lying in bed, I can see his skeleton. He is so weak that he has not been able to eat or drink much. Whatever he is able to eat or drink, he is unable to keep down. Vomiting occurs without warning. I know that our Father has given me the story of Martha, Mary, and Lazarus this morning because He wants me to know that, while His coming was delayed, He did come and Lazarus was raised. You can imagine how my mind does not stop. I am continually thinking. All day my prayers are for healing, and I am asking what I can do to make Lawrence more comfortable. When I go to bed at night I am wondering: *Will this be the night he passes in his sleep while curled up behind me? or will tomorrow morning be the morning that he jumps out of bed full of health and vigor, forgetting that he had ever been sick?* As the day continued, I finished my walk, and, while I was in the kitchen cleaning, my life flashed before me in an instant. I cannot help but think that it is the Holy Spirit who did this.

The Holy Spirit continues to draw near to Lawrence and me. It is like what happened when the three Hebrew boys were thrown into the fiery furnace—Christ was in the midst of that fire with them. He continues to be with us in the midst of this trial in the person of the Holy Spirit. He has brought back to my mind a time shortly after my first husband and I were divorced. Financially, I was struggling. My three children were small, and we were forced by circumstances to move into a bachelor apartment because I could not afford anything bigger. For one year, I had to cook on a hot plate because we did not have a kitchen, let alone a stove. During that time, a dear friend of mine, Lora Abell, who happens to be Lawrence's ex-wife, shared with me how the Lord had just blessed her and her children with a home, even though she felt unworthy. She told me that God does not bless us because we are worthy but because He can. I did not tell Lora how unworthy I was feeling at that time. I was attending church and yet feeling as if I had no place there. I felt that I could not ask God for anything because I had sinned so badly. Only those who know me and what was happening at that time know how precious it was that God would send such a message to me through Lora.

The scenes of that time continued to flood my mind. I remember how I went home that day and told my children that we were going to begin fasting and praying that the Lord would bless us with a house. We would fast for thirty days. Each one of us would give up something—television, candy, or whatever it might be. Each person decided what they wanted to give up during the fast. The end of the month was approaching, and I began to ask God what I was to do. I felt as if I should be out looking for a house, and yet I had never looked for one before. I did not know what I should do. Another week passed, and I had not found a suitable house. Finally, the last of the thirty days of seeking God for a house had come. I came home that day, went to the mailbox as I usually do, and discovered that I had received a letter from the city of Inglewood, informing me that I had been selected to receive a three-bedroom house. As you can imagine, I began screaming. My children asked what was wrong. As the tears ran down my face, I told them that God had just answered our prayers. The letter stated that I had to report to a meeting to receive the details about the house. The day of the meeting came, and, as I sat listening, I found out that HUD had just completed building several condominiums in various cities. I and about three hundred others had been selected from all of the housing applicants. To this day, I do not remember submitting an application. I have no doubt that it was God who placed my information in this selection pool. The facilitator told us at the meeting that there were only about twenty units left for the three hundred names selected, so the people who got a house would need to be determined by lottery, as names went into a bowl and were randomly selected. We were instructed to go to the various locations listed and look at the available units. Then we were to pick which location and unit we preferred. On the day of the lottery, each person was given a number. The people whose numbers were selected were to go down front and indicate which unit and location they wanted. I did as instructed. I had no doubt that my number would be among the twenty numbers that would be called. It was not by chance that I had received that letter in the mail on the very day that we had asked God to give us a house.

I need to go back for a moment and tell you something else. As my children and I began praying for a house, my children began to get excited. My oldest daughter thought it would be a great idea to put in her special request for this house. She wanted a three-bedroom house so that she could have her own room. She also wanted the house to have an upstairs and a downstairs.

Chapter 6. Nearer Still Nearer

I stopped her at that point and told her that Mommy had to be able to afford the house, so we should not ask God for such an elaborate one. I did not know it at the time, but God was about to show me just how mighty He truly is. Why do we continue to limit God's ability to keep His Word? He tells us in 1 John 5:14, 15: "And this is the confidence that we have in him, that, if we ask any thing according to his will, he heareth us: And if we know that he hear us, whatsoever we ask, we know that we have the petitions that we desired of him."

I did as we were instructed and went to the location that I desired to have. I walked in and was amazed to find that it was a three-bedroom house, with an upstairs and downstairs. There had been a few requests that I secretly wanted, but I was afraid to ask God for them. I had not even spoken this desire to anyone. At the time, I really wanted to have a stainless steel kitchen sink. As I walked into the kitchen, I was amazed to see that it had a stainless steel sink. Besides wanting a stainless steal sink, I was concerned about yard work and safety. I did not want to come in at night with no one around. God had read my thoughts and knew my fears. Because the HUD houses were condominiums, they were gated and the yards were maintained by the association. The only words that come to my mind now and then are: WHAT A MIGHTY GOD WE SERVE!

> *God had read my thoughts and knew my fears.*

How could anyone ever say that this was all a coincidence? Can you see how our God works out circumstances for our good? Even when we do not deserve it, He continually shows us that He loves us. In my journal, I wrote:

> God spoke to me this morning after He reminded me of His wonderful love for us and His mercy and ability to provide for our needs. He wanted me to know that it might not appear that He has heard my request, though He has. He wanted me to know that, in His time, He would answer. He repeated my husband's words to me: "Hold On."
>
> We learn from 1 John 5:14, 15, that we can be confident in our God yet we must ask all things according to His will.

If we do this, He will hear us. We can make our requests known to Him, for He wants to give us the desires of our hearts. "Therefore I say unto you, What things soever ye desire, when ye pray, believe that ye receive them, and ye shall have them" (Mark 11:24). To pray that God's will might be done in our lives, we must believe that God loves us. We must believe that, in spite of what we request, God knows best. If He sees that our request is not for our good, we must give Him permission not to grant it. We must ask God to give us what *He* sees best for our lives and for our salvation.

On the day that we had to report back for the drawing, I walked into the room with confidence that it was God's desire to give my children and me that house. It had every detail of our spoken and unspoken requests. I forgot to tell you that my fear of affording such a house was taken care of as well. Because this was a HUD project, the houses were being sold based on the individual buyer's income. So there was no doubt that I would be able to afford it.

The facilitator started calling the names. As you might have guessed by now, I got the house! My name was the third to be called. As I walked forward to give my information to the person up front, the tears began to flow. I have no idea what the person was thinking as I stood sobbing while giving her my information. On the inside, I was praising God, thanking Him for the mercy that He had showed me in spite of my unfaithfulness to Him. Our Father was willing to grant me this precious gift.

While I went through the process of purchasing the house, several "road blocks" developed. However, as each was clearing, I did not worry. God had showed me how mighty He is. I knew that there was nothing that He could not do for me. I trusted at every turn that He would work it out, and He did. I lived in that house for sixteen years until Lawrence and I moved to Oroville, California. My son purchased the house, and he is now raising his family there.

The last thing Lawrence said to me the morning we were to begin the program with the medical missionary was, "I trust God, and I believe that He loves me. He loves all of us. I trust that God loves me."

The Bible is full of God's promises to us. In Philippians 4:19, we read: "But my God shall supply all your need according to his riches in glory by Christ Jesus." God wants us to daily dwell on His promises to us. He wants us to hide them in our hearts and always remember that, "according to all that he promised: there hath not failed one word of all his good promise" (1 Kings 8:56).

Satan wants me to become discouraged and sad. Christ tells me, "Hold on, for I have showed you that I can do many and mighty things for you. I will continue to do these mighty things on your behalf." My response to Him is that I *will* hold on.

One of the statements of Ellen G. White that Lawrence has repeated when talking of God's mercy is: "God speaks to His people in blessings bestowed; and when these are not appreciated, He speaks to them in blessings removed, that they may be led to see their sins, and return to Him with all the heart" (*Patriarchs and Prophets*, p. 470). We must remember that God's one purpose is to save us. He is so true to His purpose that He sent His only begotten Son to die for us. By this precious gift of a house that fulfilled my daughter's specifications, God won my heart to Him in a special way. I knew that, even though I had failed Him, He was still my God and He loved me. I was determined to serve Him and trust Him more than ever.

> *I knew that, even though I had failed Him, He was still my God and He loved me.*

"Blessings bestowed" had won my heart.

This morning, the Holy Spirit continues to bring before my mind past blessings. He is now reminding me of how He blessed us with the current house we are living in.

I can remember how I loved Southern California. All of my family is there. I was born and raised there. Although I had heard many, many messages on the importance of moving out of the big cities, in my heart I knew that I never wanted to leave. The weather was perfect; everything I needed was there.

One Sabbath, Lawrence, his brother Jerold, and I went to another seminar on the importance of moving out of the big cities. I remember coming home that afternoon and saying to them both, "I have to be honest, I don't want to leave Los Angeles. If I'm going to leave, God is going to have to change my heart. God knows my heart, and I don't have the desire to leave." Time passed, and we did not speak of it again that I can remember. One year later, I cannot tell you what happened, nor can I tell you when it happened. All I know is that God changed my heart. I woke up one day, and I heard myself saying these words to Lawrence: "It is time for us to go. We should start making plans to leave." I must stop here to say again that God loves us very much. All He asks of us is to have a willing spirit. He knows our difficulties, and He knows our struggles. If we would only place these difficulties and struggles at the feet of Jesus and present to Him a willing heart to be changed, He will do the work in us. The sooner we understand that we can do *nothing* apart from Jesus, the sooner we will begin to stay at the feet of Jesus, waiting to be molded into what He wants us to be.

> *He knows our difficulties, and He knows our struggles. If we would only place these difficulties and struggles at the feet of Jesus and present to Him a willing heart to be changed, He will do the work in us.*

Once I announced that it was time to go, we began letting our family in Northern California know about our plans of moving there. This is where we had always said we would move if we ever left the big city. That is where Lawrence's family was. My sister-in-law Shirley told us on one of our visits, "There is a house that you just have to go by and see. It is a beautiful house with three levels and an

Chapter 6. Nearer Still Nearer

elevator, and it sits right on the bluff overlooking Oroville." Lawrence was very reluctant to even see the house. He knew from their description that we could not afford it. "Why would we tempt ourselves," he said. "We can't afford it." My response was a typical Brenda response, "I know we can't afford it, but it won't hurt us to see the house." I told him that our Father owns everything and that, if He wants us to have it, it will be ours. He refused a few more times until his mother jumped into the conversation and said that she was curious to see the house. At that, he gave in, and Shirley made the arrangements for us to see the house.

As the realtor showed us the house, I was in awe of its beauty. Immediately I noticed that the kitchen counters had a tiled backsplash. That is a feature that I had said I wanted my next house to have. The realtor proceeded to take us to the second level. As we got to the third level, which was a huge garage with a very high sealing, I received a very strong impression that this was to be *my* house. I turned to the agent and said, "This is my house. God had this house built for me." The agent looked at me puzzled, not knowing how to respond to my comment. Then he proceeded to show us the rest of the house.

While touring the house, I envisioned just how perfect this house was for us. You see, Lawrence and I had decided that we would reopen our catering business when he retired. This house has a beautiful 40x40 deck overlooking Oroville. I could see having wonderful outdoor events there. The third level, as I said, is a huge 40x40 garage, which I would have converted into a multipurpose room for indoor events when the weather did not permit going outside. The second level has two bedrooms with a kitchen, a bathroom with laundry hook ups, and a living room area. The top floor is one bedroom, living room, kitchen, and one and a half bathrooms. There is also a deck off the bedroom and living room. From the bedroom and the living room, there is a panoramic view of Oroville that is simply breathtaking. I knew Lawrence was right about our not being able to afford it, but I also knew, without a doubt, that it was God who had given me my first house. I also knew that the Holy Spirit had given me a strong impression that this house was to be ours. So, as far as I was concerned, I was going to move forward until the Lord showed me otherwise.

I told the realtor that I would get back with him. Lawrence and I went home to Gardena, California. Once there, Lawrence reviewed his retirement benefits and discovered that it would be best if he waited a few more years to maximize his benefits. For three months, I worked on my husband, trying to convince him that we could afford the house.

Each month I called the realtor to let him know that I was still convincing my husband to purchase the house. Our expenses were very low in Gardena. We were still living in the house that God had blessed my children and me with. The monthly mortgage was extremely low because of the special HUD housing program I had received. In addition, we now had two incomes, so I felt that we could purchase the house and that it would be waiting for us when we were ready to move. Three months had passed, and Lawrence would not budge on his decision about the house. Yet, you know how ladies can be. When our husbands do not see things as we do, we go to work on them. In this instance, however, it did not work, and my husband was not budging. I made my monthly call to the realtor, and, this time, he told me that the house had just sold. My heart sank! I was sure that God had told me that this was to be *our* house. As I placed the phone back on the receiver, I found myself saying, "Oh well, I trust that the perfect house will be there for us when we are ready to move." After that, I did not give the house another thought. I had learned that I could trust my wants and my desires to God. If something does not work out the way I think it should, that is just fine. I don't want anything that God does not want for me. I think it is important that we understand that our heavenly Father knows everything

CHAPTER 6. NEARER STILL NEARER

from beginning to end. Even though we have worked out in our minds how something should be

> *I don't want anything that God does not want for me.*

and it all seems to be for the good, our prayer must always be: "Nevertheless, not my will, but thine, be done." With this as our prayer, we can let go of things when they appear not to be working out the way we planned, and we can trust that God is working out circumstances for our good. Such belief about our Lord and Saviour gives us peace that passes all understanding. "And the peace of God, which passeth all understanding, shall keep your hearts and minds through Christ Jesus" (Phil. 4:7).

Three years passed before Lawrence decided that it was time for him to retire and we could move to Northern California. So many things took place in those three years. Our plans changed from restarting our catering business to running a care home for the elderly. Lawrence and I were now caring for three elderly family members of mine. With both of us working full-time jobs, it was challenging to care for them. During those three years, the Lord showed us that there are now six-bed residential care homes. These are homes that are licensed by the state to care for the elderly. We decided to open one when we moved up north, allowing us to help care for our family as well as supplement Lawrence's retirement.

We revealed our plans to our family in Northern California. Shirley, my sister-in-law, was working at a hospital lab at the time. She learned from a patient about a friend of his who was looking to sell a care home that he owned. Shirley called us right away to let us know. However, she and Lawrence's brother Rufus were also thinking about opening a care home, so she would keep me posted about their plans. I remember thinking, as I hung up the phone: *If this care home is for us, the Lord will work it out.* A few days later, Shirley called to tell us that they had decided against opening a care home and that she would make arrangements for us to come up and meet with the people wanting to sell their business.

Lawrence and I drove up to meet with the couple, and we came away amazed at how well the meeting went. It was as if we had known one another for years. They were from Romania and planned to move back to their country. They both loved the Lord and wanted to make sure that whoever bought their care home loved the Lord too. We found out later that they had not planned on selling their care home just then. Their plan was to move back to Romania in another two to three years, and they were still in the planning process. However, after meeting with us, they concluded that it was to Lawrence and me that they wanted to sell their care home. Everything fell into place. Within three months, Lawrence and I had purchased the business, obtained licensing from the state, and completed our administrator's classes. Because it was God's plan for us, every door opened. Everything went smoothly.

Originally, we had planned to add a few rooms to the existing care home so that we could live on site with my aunt and my grandmother, for whom we were caring. However, half way through the purchasing process, I received a strong impression that we should purchase another place to live. It was my plan to eventually own three six-bed facilities, and, by purchasing a separate place for us to live, in time we could get that home licensed as well and begin expanding our business. I told Lawrence what the Holy Spirit had impressed me with, and he thought it was a good idea. We began looking for a place for us to live. Almost immediately the Holy Spirit began telling me to go by the house that we had seen three years earlier. As I told you, I knew that the house had sold, and it did not make sense that a person would move into such a beautiful house and move out just three years later, so I chose to ignore the Holy Spirit's promptings. I did not even tell Lawrence what the Spirit was telling me. You see, several weeks into the purchase of the business, we had realized that the house that we had looked at three years before was just up the street and around the corner from the care home that we were in the process of purchasing. Knowing that the house had sold, we never drove by to look at it. Isn't it something how we tend to rationalize things in these little minute brains of ours instead of choosing to listen to and act on the guidance of the Holy Spirit without questioning?

Every weekend, Lawrence and I would drive up and look for housing suitable for us. It was important to us that we find a house with room for my grandmother and aunt, with privacy for Lawrence and me. We searched in all the cities surrounding Oroville and were unable to find anything suitable. The Holy Spirit continued to tell me to go by the house I had liked so much, and I continued to ignore His prompting. Lawrence and I decided that we would visit some other six-bed facilities in the area for pointers on how to run our facility. We located a care home in Paradise, about forty minutes away from where we were purchasing our business. We contacted the owners and made arrangements to go and speak with them. The experience was amazing. It was as if we had known the couple that ran it for years. During our visit, we happened to mention that we were looking for a place to live, and they told us about a house they were selling. We told them that we had put all our money into buying the business, so we would need to lease with an option to buy. They were more than willing to offer such an arrangement to us. We went by to see the house they had for sale, and it was perfect. It was a house with two levels. One could be for my grandmother and aunt and the other for Lawrence and me. The couple needed to talk to their realtor, and they would get back with us. The next day they called and informed us that the realtor had advised against a lease with an option to buy. So, our search continued. The next time we went up to scout for housing, Lawrence's youngest daughter told us about a gentleman at church who was selling his house. The house was about fifteen minutes from the care home. We went to meet with him and found the house to be just what we needed. It also had two levels, allowing us to have our privacy while being close enough to assist my aunt and grandmother. Again, we explained our situation concerning our money being tied up with the purchase of the business. We told the owner that we needed to lease with an option to buy, and he was very willing to do this. The amount he wanted for the lease was well within our budget. We left the house feeling very hopeful. He told us that he would speak to his realtor and get back with us. Later that afternoon, he called us to say that, because the house was being sold as the result of a divorce, it could not be sold as a lease option. We were both disappointed, but we trusted that God would have the perfect house for us in His time.

Nonetheless, time was running out. We were fast approaching the deadline for us to take over the business. The couple from whom we had acquired the business had purchased tickets for a vacation in Hawaii. Lawrence and I had begun discussing provisional plans to leave my aunt and grandmother in Los Angeles with family until we were able to find a house for the four of us. We would come up to Oroville and take over the business while staying with his brother Rufus and his wife. All the while, the Holy Spirit continued to prompt me to go by the house I was so interested in before, and I continued to ignore Him.

There were two weeks left before we had to take over the business in Oroville, and we still had not found a house in which to live. On our way home, we had to drop off some papers at the care home. As we got into the car to leave, once again the Holy Spirit urged me to go by the house we had seen three years earlier. I stopped the car, looked at Lawrence, and said, "Honey, the Holy Spirit has been telling me for some time now to go by the house we saw three years ago. Would you mind if we drove by the house before we get on the freeway?" Of course he did not mind, and we drove by the house. To our amazement, there was a "for sale" sign in front of the house. We looked at each other and smiled the biggest of smiles. Could it really be that, after three years, God was going to give me the house that I was so sure He had told me would be mine?

I could not wait until Monday morning to call the number listed on the "for sale" sign. Monday morning came, and I placed the call. I told the person who answered why I was calling—that we were relocating from Southern California, had just purchased a business, and were not able to buy another house. However, we wanted to know if the owner would be interested in a lease with an option to buy. The person on the line told me that the owner of the house had recently died from cancer and that the house was part of an estate sale. He informed me that a lease with an option to buy was not possible because the family wanted to liquidate all the assets of the estate right away. As I started to hang up the phone, I felt the same disappointment that I had felt three years before. Yet, before the phone hit the receiver, the Holy Spirit told me: "When you go back into town next weekend, go straight to the real estate agency and talk to them in person." I told Lawrence what had happened and what the Holy Spirit told me. When we got into town the following weekend, we went straight to the real estate office. I asked to speak with the realtor who was handling the property. We met with a woman named Nena and explained our circumstances. She listened patiently then asked if we wanted to see the house. I told her that that would not be necessary. I had seen the house three years prior and could describe the house to her. Lawrence laughed as he insisted, "You don't remember what the house looks like." I began describing the house to both of them. I talked about the kitchen, the bedroom, and the walk-in closet. I described how the bathroom was attached to the bedroom and the bookshelf that was just outside the bathroom. Nena looked at Lawrence and said, "She *does* remember the house!" Then she went on to tell us the same thing that the agent had told me on the phone, adding that the property was held by a large company, T. J. Holdings, and that they were sticklers for the rules and did not make exceptions. However, Nena concluded that it wouldn't hurt to ask. We left her office and decided that we would continue looking for other housing since this was our last trip up before we would take over the business the following weekend. Nena said that she would call us as soon as she had gotten an answer. Two days passed, and we were approaching Sabbath. That meant that our searching for a house was over. Once the Sabbath hours would begin, we would not continue to look and we had to leave for Los Angeles early Sunday morning. We confirmed our plans with Rufus and Shirley of staying with them until we were able to find a house. Moments before the sun was to set and we were to begin worship, the phone rang. It was Nena. She gave us the good news that the people whom she spoke with regarding the house were willing to lease us the house with option to buy for one year. Then she added, "Brenda, I don't understand this next part, but they wanted me to tell you that, if you and Lawrence are not able to carry a loan on the house for yourselves after the first year, they would be willing to carry the house for you until you are able to finance it on your own." I asked her how much they wanted for the monthly rent and found out that the amount was a couple hundred dollars more than we had planned, yet a portion of the monthly rent would be held and applied to the down payment. I understood why it was that Nena could not understand what had just happened, yet I could understand. My wonderful, loving, merciful, patient, caring and all-providing Father in heaven had honored a promise that He had given me three years before. The impression that I had when the realtor first showed us the house was correct. That house had been built for me. God knew what was ahead for us. He knew that, when we moved to Oroville, we would have my aunt and my grandmother with us, and He knew that the care home that we would be opening would be right around the corner from that very house. He knew that this house would be perfect for our second care home. The following weekend, we came up with all of our belongings and family and moved into our new house.

During the following months, several people would stop and comment about the house. They told us how they had watched the house being built. They told us how only the best materials were used. It only confirmed what I had already known: When God does something, He does it right. Our God owns everything; this world is His. If He sees that what you are requesting is for your good and if He sees that He can grant it and be glorified in doing so, He will give it to you. If God does not give it to me, I don't want it. If God does not give it to you, you should not want it. Put your life into the hands of God, and He will take care of you. Yes, He will take care of you.

Can you see how I almost missed this amazing blessing because, for over a month, I refused to follow the promptings of the Holy Spirit? How many blessings have I passed by because I would not listen and follow? How many blessings have you missed? How many things have been more difficult than they needed to be because we would not trust the still, small voice when we were told to do or not to do something? Lawrence and I searched for over a month for a house and God had our house waiting for us. I just would not listen as He told me: "Go by the house."

This morning, God, in His mercy, is reminding me how He has worked for me in the past and of my decision to trust Him even when it appears that things are not working out the way I had planned. He is showing me that, right now, He wants me to have the peace that passes all understanding, even though there has been no improvement in Lawrence's health (Phil. 4:7). Lawrence gets weaker and weaker by the day. God is reminding me that He is forever working on our behalf even when we do not see it.

As I travel through this very, very difficult time, I am holding onto the hand of Jesus and trusting that He is with us. Even though I am not getting the answer that I desire, God, in His infinite mercy, reminds me to hold on and be patient. He reminds me how He has blessed me and provided for me in the past. He reminds me that I can trust Him with my deepest desires. He reminds me that, if the answer appears to be "no," I should accept His "no" and believe that what He has for me is better than anything I could want for myself.

After receiving the news that the house was ours that Sabbath evening, I hung up the phone. As we knelt to pray, I could not speak. The tears began to flow like a river. I was overwhelmed with the love that my God had for me. I was in awe at how He had orchestrated the circumstances of my life from the moment I spoke those first words, "If I am going to leave the city, God is going to have to change my heart." This one simple act of giving my heart to God to do with what He willed resulted in a wonderful miracle. This was not because I was worthy, for I could never be worthy of His grace. He did it because He loves us so much. That is why He blesses us—He wants us with Him. We can trust Him with our lives even when things do not seem to be going right. It is God, and God alone, who can and will cause all things to work together for the good of those who love God and are called according to his purpose (Rom. 8:28). That evening I cried tears of thanksgiving to Jesus Christ our Saviour for this awesome and wonderful and mighty blessing. Lawrence and I could never have afforded this house. We still cannot afford this house. Yet, God has not only given us a business to pay for it, but He has also sustained that business so that we can afford the payments and maintenance of the house. He chose to bless us in being able to open a second care home, and He has continued to provide us with the residents to keep the business running. In this economy, we have watched how one business after another has had to close its doors, and yet we are still open and running. We know that this is done only through the mercies of our loving Father in heaven.

In the midst of my despair this morning, my precious Savior has drawn so close to me once again. He has comforted me as He reminds me of how He has been faithful in the past to provide for me. He has reminded me how He has heard my spoken and unspoken requests and was faithful to grant them. He has shown me that I can be confident that He will grant my current request as well, according to His purpose and will, in His time. As I ponder His delay, watching and waiting for Him to touch my husband's body and heal him, the Father is telling me, "Hold on, Brenda, I am doing a work. Be patient, be patient."

JOURNAL ENTRY: *"No Improvement"*

As it has to do with Lawrence's illness, each day continues to duplicate the day before. We are not seeing any improvement. He is becoming weaker and weaker. His vomiting has increased over the past few days. We thought that, because he has been unable to eat or drink, he was starting to have symptoms of dehydration. I contacted his doctor to find out if there is any way that we can get fluids into him. We were told that arrangements could be made for him to come in and receive fluids in the clinic in which chemotherapy is given. The family is very hopeful. We believe that once he gets the fluids, he will gain strength, and that once he has gotten a little strength back, he will be able to go forward with the program that the medical missionary laid out for us. I will take Lawrence in tomorrow for fluids.

Lawrence has had two days of fluids, and, to our disappointment, the fluids did not help. In fact, when the fluids went in, he immediately started vomiting, and the vomiting continued through the night once we got home. On Thursday, September 6, 2012, I sent the following fax to his doctor:

Dr. Potter,

I am sorry for being such a bother this week but I am just not sure if I am doing all I can and should be doing for my husband. As you know, we are not able to stop the vomiting. He has come in for fluids and nausea medication, and, while they are putting in the medication, he is vomiting. I have used the suppositories, and they are not working either. Yesterday, he vomited three times while in your office and once at home. He vomited until 1:00 a.m. He had a few hours rest, and it began again at 4:30 a.m. Any talking or movement brings it on.

I am sure that, because of the cancer in his liver, the bowel gases are building up. If you could please call me and let me know what the CT scan from Paradise Hospital showed.

Yesterday, Craig, the nurse in your office, told me about a program that is done out of the home for IV fluids and nutrition. Is this program part of the hospice program? Is there any way that we could have Lawrence referred to this program?

One of Lawrence's daughters is a trauma nurse at UCLA, and she wanted me to ask if it would be possible for Lawrence to have a bowel drain. She also feels that the body fluids are not able to be processed from the body fast enough, and that is why he is not able to stop the vomiting.

I am sorry. I know that you have a lot of patients. I just do not know what I should do.

Thank you.

The doctor's response to my fax was that he wanted me to bring Lawrence in to see him on Friday, September 7, if he were able to handle the drive.

That evening, while I was helping Lawrence to get into the shower, he told me that he felt it was time to call hospice. I was shocked at the announcement. Running a care home, I am very familiar with hospice. I know that calling hospice does not necessarily mean the end is near; it just means that you have decided to let nature take its course, that you will no longer continue to try to delay death, which is inevitably going to happen. He knew, as I knew, that he was continuing to decline. As the days went by for me and Lawrence did not improve, I convinced myself that God was going to wait until the final hour before He raised Lawrence from his bed of illness. I had no doubt that he would be healed. I even entertained the idea, because the healing had not yet taken place, that maybe the Lord was going to perform a Lazarus-type of miracle. Maybe God saw that He would be glorified in a mightier way if Lawrence were raised from the dead. I have no doubt that God has the power to do just that.

I asked Lawrence if he felt we should try to take him to one of the places that treats terminal cancer, such as the Cancer Treatment Centers of America. His response to me was "no." He said that he would not do anything that would show distrust or lack of acceptance of God's decision. I told him that we were scheduled to see his doctor the next day and that we could discuss hospice with him at that time. I was able to keep my emotions in check long enough to help Lawrence complete his shower. Once he was back in bed and resting, I left the room and went into the kitchen, as I would do whenever I had to cry. I barely made it out of the room when the tears began to flow. I must have cried for an hour or more. When I returned to the room, Lawrence told me that he was so sorry. He had heard me crying. He was sorry that everything was falling on me. I explained that I had not intended that he hear me, but he had to know that, because I love him so much, I could not help but cry at times. I explained that I was trying to be strong for him, but, sometimes, I just needed to cry. I was so sorry that he heard me. It was early in the evening. However, whenever things were too heavy for either of us to bear, we would curl up next to each other, and, for us, all would be right in our world. And that is what we did.

JOURNAL ENTRY: *September 7, 2012*

It is Friday, September 7, 2012. I woke up this morning at 4:00 a.m. with the words, "Nearer my God to thee.

Nearer still nearer, nearer to thee," continually coming to my mind. Over and over these words were repeated in my head. I was not able to get back to sleep because of these words, which the Lord has brought to my mind. I know that His desire is to draw me nearer to Him and that He has indeed drawn nearer to me. I believe, however, that He is telling me that He is drawing even nearer to Lawrence and me right now. Could it be that He is about to raise my husband from his bed of affliction?

A few weeks back, when we were first beginning our journey with the medical missionary, the Lord began comforting me with phrases from hymns. The first words that came to me were: "What a friend we have in Jesus, oh what needless pain we bear, all because we do not carry everything to God in prayer." I knew, at that time, that the Holy Spirit was telling me that I was carrying a burden that I did not need to carry. He was letting me know that He is my friend and that I should lay this before Him in prayer. Certainly I have been praying all along, but I was not fully trusting God with this. I was afraid to give it to Him because I was afraid that His answer might be to not heal Lawrence. Our gentle, precious Savior began showing me how to truly release this to Him. He began reminding me, from the beginning, how faithful He had been to me throughout my life. He had begun helping me to die to self and give this completely over to Him. I know firsthand of all the ways that the Lord worked with me, comforted me, spoke to me, and held my hand. Lawrence was not able to talk much after we returned from Loma Linda because of the pain he was having, but, when we did talk, I knew that the Lord had drawn especially close to him as well. We talked about how we both felt God's presence with us in a special way before we left for Loma Linda. In addition, while we were in Loma Linda, we talked often about how good God had been to us. We both felt God's presence around us in a different, closer way. We didn't know, at the time, what was about to take place. We just knew that God had come close to us. We felt His presence in a way that we had not felt before, and for that we were truly grateful.

The peace I saw in Lawrence the last few weeks of his life, however, was a different type of peace. My husband was a very quiet and gentle man, but the peace he now exhibited was one I had never seen before. I could understand this peace myself because God was walking with me as He was walking with my husband.

JOURNAL ENTRY: *"Receiving the News"*

We went in to see the doctor today as planned. The doctor informed us that there was nothing else that could be done for Lawrence. The cancer had all but completely taken over his liver. His body could not process anything. Jaimie, Lawrence's daughter, was conferenced in by phone. As she spoke with the doctor to discuss different options, Lawrence sat quietly listening. After all options were exhausted, Jaimie asked her father if he understood what the doctor was telling him. Lawrence answered, "Yes," and did not appear to be the least bit upset or concerned. His countenance showed absolute resolve. When the doctor left the room, we were alone for a few moments. At first there was silence, and then he said to me, "Brenda, you're gonna have to be strong now if we are going to be together when Christ comes." He went on to say that he was now going to be praying for the family and me. I truly believe from those few words that he spoke that he knew that God had accepted him; he knew that he was covered with the blood of his precious Saviour. He had prayed all the prayers that he could on his own behalf. During the time he had left, he would pray for the loved ones that he was leaving behind.

As I reflect back on that morning, I remember the Holy Spirit waking me at 4:00 a.m. and bringing the words to my mind: "Nearer my God to thee." Now I have the truest understanding of what was taking place that morning. God knew what news we were going to receive that day. So, in the early morning hours, His Spirit came to let me know that He had drawn even closer to us. God was telling me that He had begun drawing still nearer to Lawrence and me. I just did not know why. I was witnessing the Saviour carrying my husband in that doctor's office as he received the news that they had done all that could be done. I heard the same news that Lawrence had just heard, and yet there was a peace within me. I was not afraid. Yes, I was still holding onto the hope that Christ would step in during the final hours and raise my husband, but I also knew that, if He decided not to, I would accept His answer. Christ had given both of us peace that passes all understanding (Phil. 4:7). What a precious gift—to know that we were not alone during our darkest hours! The picture of the three Hebrew boys in that fiery furnace comes to my mind (read Daniel 3:8–30). Just as Christ came down in the midst of the fire to be with them, He had come down to be with Lawrence and me. I love you, Jesus!

As I received the final answer from God in the matter through the words of the physician, Christ was drawing nearer to Lawrence and me. We both received the peace that passes all understanding that day. There was no fear. I must admit that I still had not fully accepted that the answer was "no." I told Lawrence, when he said that he wanted me to be strong, that I would be strong. However, I told him that I would not accept that God would not raise him until he had been in the grave three days. I knew that Lazarus had been raised after three days. I truly believed, and still believe, that, if God would be glorified by Lawrence's resurrection, He would and could do so. As David pleaded with God to save his child, I would plead with God to raise my husband. For me, the doctors did not have the last say—my Father did.

Lawrence quietly listened to my rantings as we sat in the doctor's office, and, without any real response to what I had said, he asked if there were a place that he could lay

Chapter 6. Nearer Still Nearer

down for awhile before we started the ride home. It had taken so much out of him making that trip to the doctor. My husband was a wise man. He knew that I needed to hold onto the hope until the very end that God was going to raise him, and he allowed me to do just that—to hold on.

My practice was to go over to Lawrence's side of the bed and ask if there were anything he needed before I got into bed. On Friday, September 7, when I asked him that question, he looked at me with excitement on his face and in his voice and said, "Brenda, God is going to answer my prayer!"

I remember hesitating for a moment. In my mind I was thinking: *I only know of one prayer that he has shared with me and that was that he had prayed that God would allow him to go to sleep if God was not going to raise him from this illness.* I looked at him and I said matter-of-factly, "Yes, I know." You see, I knew what the doctors had said to us that day, but the doctors did not think it would happen so quickly, and you know what I was praying for. So, I felt I still had more time. I felt that God was waiting for the final hour to perform His miracle. I realize now that God must have let Lawrence know that He was going to let him go to sleep, and, like the first night he prayed that prayer, Lawrence was telling me so I would not be shocked or scared. He wanted me to know what was about to take place, and I missed it. I wish so very much that I would have had the insight to ask Lawrence what he felt at that moment. Oh, I believe I know what he felt—he was happy. I know this because of how he told me that God was going to answer his prayer. It was with excitement. Yet, it would have been nice for me to hear him express it in words.

It is hard for me to explain to you the extreme closeness we were both feeling to our heavenly Father. The presence of death was all around us and yet there was no fear. I guess it was best said by David, "Yea, though I walk through the valley of the shadow of death, I will fear no evil: for thou art with me; thy rod and thy staff they comfort me" (Psalm 23:4). David added, "My cup runneth over." That is how I am feeling right now. My cup runneth over. Lawrence and I actually experienced first hand what David is saying here. There was no fear for we knew that Christ was with us. He had begun drawing even nearer than He had been before. On Thursday, September 7, when He woke me at 4:00 a.m., God was telling me, with the words, "Nearer my God to thee. Nearer still nearer, nearer to thee," that He was drawing even nearer. For two days, I was comforted with these words. I know that God was being gracious and loving to me, and I have no doubt that He was speaking to Lawrence as well.

It is so important that you understand just how much our heavenly Father loves you. He is such a tender, patient, and loving God. He stands near with His arms stretched out to you, longing for you to come to Him, to trust in Him, and to believe and obey Him. "Yet God is ever seeking to instruct finite men, that they may exercise faith in him, and trust themselves wholly in his hands. Every drop of rain or flake of snow, every spear of grass, every leaf and flower and shrub, testifies of God. These little things, so common around us, teach the lesson that nothing is beneath the notice of the infinite God, nothing is too small for His attention" (*Healthful Living*, p. 294).

Can you not see that your life could and would be a never-ending love story that unfolds day by day if you only turn your life over to the Father completely? There is nothing that we cannot trust Him with. He has walked in our shoes, and He knows our struggles. His desire is that we not struggle alone. Do you remember the first song that I told you the Holy Spirit brought to my mind? It was, "What a friend we have in Jesus. Oh, what needless pain we bear—all because we do not carry everything to God in prayer."

Whatever your struggle in life, turn it over to the Father. He can and will handle it. You will find that you have the peace of the everlasting Father within you because you know that it is His struggle and not yours. Trust in His wisdom to see you through. Let your prayer be the prayer of Christ when He walked the earth: "Not my will, but thine, be done."

Lawrence's favorite phrase the last few years of his life was: "Hold on, hold on." I am pleading with you to grab the hand of Jesus and hold on.

CHAPTER 7. *Saying Good-bye*

It was Sabbath, September 8. Again, the words, "Nearer my God to thee," kept coming to my mind. Over and over, throughout the day, these words kept coming to my mind. "Nearer my God to thee, nearer still nearer, nearer to thee." How precious is our Saviour! He was drawing nearer to me that day. God knew what I would face, and He was letting me know that I was not alone.

I noticed a big change in Lawrence when he woke up today. He was no longer able to sit up on the side of the bed. After Friday's news, family who were out of town heard that it was time for them to come to see Lawrence. Arrangements were made for his youngest daughter, Tracie, and her children to fly in. Steven and Mary were able to arrive by early Saturday evening and able to spend time with Lawrence. Jerold and Veronica did not get into town until after midnight. They decided that they would rest and come see Lawrence on Sunday morning.

Family members left our home at 10:00 p.m., and I went in to prepare for bed. As usual, I went over to Lawrence's side of the bed and asked if there were anything he needed. He asked that I get him some ice chips. He ate a few of them, and I noticed his breathing was beginning to get very labored. As it became even more labored, I called his daughter Jaime, who is a nurse at UCLA Medical Center. I put the phone next to Lawrence so she could hear him. She informed me that we had to slow down his breathing or he would have a heart attack. For hours, Jaime and I worked to get his breathing to slow down. As she gave instructions, I would carry them out on my end. It was 2:00 a.m. when his breathing finally slowed down. I was sitting on the side of the bed, watching Lawrence, when he looked up at me and said, "Get in the bed." I asked if he was sure he was all right and he answered, "Yes," and then he motioned for me to get in the bed. As I climbed into bed and curled up behind him, he reached back and put his hand on my leg, acknowledging my presence, and then I went to sleep. Needless to say, I was exhausted. I had been up since 6:00 a.m. the previous morning, and it was now 2:00 a.m. the following day.

Suddenly I woke up. I looked at Lawrence, and he was still breathing yet quiet. I looked at the clock and it was 3:00 a.m. I decided to get out of the bed, go around, and look at him directly in the face to make sure that he was all right. It was then that I noticed his eyes did not look right. I immediately called Jaime. I explained what I was seeing. I told her that I thought that Lawrence was passing. She asked that I put the phone on speaker and hold it to his ear. I did, and she began talking to her father. She asked him, "Daddy, are you in any pain?" Lawrence shook his head "no." I told Jaime that he was responding by shaking his head "no." She asked that I put the phone back up to her father's ear, then she said to him, "Daddy, it's OK. Don't fight it daddy. Just let go. I love you daddy." When she stopped talking, I put the phone to my ear, and Jaime said to me, "I believe it is just the medicine that you are seeing." We had to give him a lot of pain medicine to slow down his breathing. I remember thinking at the time: *That was a strange thing to say to your father if you think it is just the effects of the medication*, but I explained it away to myself that she meant that he should not fight the medicine. I told her that I would call her back in a little while to let her know how he was. I hung up the phone, climbed back into bed, and curled up behind Lawrence again. As I placed my arm around him, he began to take his last three breaths. With the first breath, I knew what was happening. I continued to hold him, and I spoke these words. "I'll see you when you wake up. I'll see you when you wake up." He took his last two breaths and was gone. I know he heard and understood what I had said to him because he had just responded to his daughter Jaime.

How loving was my heavenly Father to me! I was exhausted and, by all rights, should have slept straight through until 7:00 or 8:00 a.m. that morning. I had only been asleep for an hour when I woke up. I know that it was the Holy Spirit who woke me. My Saviour knew that I would want to be awake when my husband closed his eyes for the last time. Our Saviour knew how close Lawrence and I were. There was nothing we did not do together. I know Lawrence not only wanted me with him when he died, but he wanted me awake, and I wanted to be awake. As hard as it was to lose him, it happened the way that we both wanted. Again, I say, we have a heavenly Father who cares about us, who loves us. God knew the pain I would have experienced if I had slept through my husband's last breaths. I can never repay my debt to the Father for His tender mercies to Lawrence and me. As I look back on those last weeks with Lawrence, I find myself asking how I was able to go through the motions to do the things that I did. As I pen this part of the story, it is very evident to me that it was Christ who was carrying me as I walked through this journey. It was Christ guiding my words and my actions; it was Christ leading the way. It was He who spoke to me on that ride home from Loma Linda, telling me to begin writing. He knew what He was about to do for Lawrence and me. I thank God; I thank God for loving me so!

Pastor Ivor Myers preached a sermon entitled, "A Love Story." I encourage you to go online and find it and listen to it. It carries a beautiful message. Yet, I must tell you that Lawrence and I were privileged to have our own love story, which God unfolded before our eyes. I am so proud of my husband. It was a privilege to walk this journey with him. I watched him accept God's decision in the matter with such peace, with such resolve, and with such trust. He had completely surrendered to Christ. It was Christ I saw as he carried my husband through the valley of death. The marvelous and wonderful thing about it is that Christ was carrying me at the same time. Again, I must give praise to my God. What an awesome and loving God I serve! He spent time with me as if I were the only person on earth that needed Him. I know He was with Lawrence as well—every bit as close to him as He was to me. Knowing God as I do, I know that there have been countless others who have needed Him as Lawrence and I did, and He has been with them too.

I do not know what relationship you have with God. However, I am asking you to examine whatever relationship you do have. God loves you very much. He wants you to live with Him for eternity. Please surrender to Him now. In the words of my husband, taken from one of the two sermons that he preached, "Won't you choose Him today?"

My son James was with me at the time Lawrence passed. He had flown up two weeks prior. I had no idea how much I needed him to be with me. However, God, in His infinite mercy, knew, and He had impressed my son to come and be with Lawrence and me. I thank my son James so much for his wisdom in listening to the Holy Spirit and coming. My son heard me crying when Lawrence passed and came in to assist me.

I held onto the hope that God was going to raise Lawrence from his bed of illness. Yet, all the while I prayed, "Not my will, but thine, be done" (Luke 22:42). I was willing to accept God's decision in the matter. How could I question God? He had shown us so much mercy and tender care. I cried for a while, and then I thanked Him for answering my husband's prayer.

Satan's Double Attack

After I was able to gather my emotions, I called Lawrence's mother to inform her that Lawrence had passed away. I wanted to know if Jerold and Veronica wanted to come and see Lawrence before the coroner took him away. They got in so late that they were unable to see him before he died. My mother-in-law put me on hold and went to wake Jerold and Veronica to see what they wanted to do. She knocked on the door for a few moments, and no one answered, so she came back to the phone and told me that she would call back as soon as she was able to wake one of them.

The next call I received was from my sister-in-law Shirley. She was frantic. All she kept repeating was: "Start praying for Veronica! Start praying for Veronica—they can't wake her up!" She then was able to get out that she was on her way to Mom's house and that she would call me back as soon as she knew more.

I began praying. I could not wrap my head around what was happening. I had just lost my husband. What could be happening? A short while passed and my phone rang again. This time one of my children answered, and I could here them saying that Veronica was dead. I began to cry out, and, in a split second, I could feel the Holy Spirit impress upon my mind that Satan was responsible for this attack. Satan was determined to shake the faith of this family. Immediately, I was impressed to stop crying out, and I began to repeat these words: "Satan, you are a liar. You will not shake our faith in God. Satan, you will not cause us to doubt God." Then, I began to pray silently.

Needless to say, it would be several hours before the family could come to my side for comforting. They were at my mother-in-law's house dealing with the sudden death of Veronica. We had lost two of our family members within moments of one another. Jerold not only lost a brother, but, in the same hour, he also lost his wife. In the months following Lawrence and Veronica's deaths, all that came out of my mouth when it opened were praises to God. As sad as I am for my loss, God has been so gracious! He has opened my eyes that I might see His tender mercies.

I have already explained how Lawrence's quick death was a direct answer to his prayer. Yet, as for Veronica, let me explain just how merciful God was to her and Jerold.

Several years back, both Jerold and Veronica moved to Yucca Valley to care for her parents. Her father passed away a few years before Lawrence's illness, so, by now, they were only caring for her mother. Her mother has high-level Alzheimer's. She currently resides in a care home. Veronica and Jerold do not have any other family in Yucca Valley. Some of Veronica's cousins live a few hours away, but none of Jerold's family is close.

I truly, truly believe that God, in His infinite wisdom, was watching tenderly over His children Veronica and Jerold. He saw what Satan had in store for them. He knew that Veronica was about to die and also knew the way in which she would die. I could just hear Him saying, "All right, Satan, I see what you have in store for my children. I am going to work out the circumstance in such a way in that my son Jerold will be able to handle it." In His Word, God tells us: "There hath no temptation taken you but such as is common to man: but God is faithful, who will not suffer you to be tempted above that ye are able; but will with the temptation also make a way to escape, that ye may be able to bear it" (1 Cor. 10:13).

God carefully orchestrated events. He timed them perfectly. He sustained Veronica until she was able to get to Northern California, where Jerold would be surrounded by his family. Then God gently began laying Lawrence to sleep, which provided the motivation for Jerold and Veronica coming up north in the first place. There could be no better possible explanation for the timing of these two deaths. The doctors told us that they expected Lawrence to die but they did not expect it to happen so quickly. It was not even a full forty-eight hours after leaving the doctor's office that Lawrence was gone. Jerold shared with us that Veronica had been having symptoms all week. He had tried to get her to the doctor, and she refused. We know now that Veronica was going to have a massive heart attack, based on the information we have received since her death. However, it was God who sustained her until they were able to get to Oroville, where Jerold would have his family to hold him up. God knew that we could handle losing them both. Satan was seeking to destroy our family's faith in God, but God knew that we would draw closer to Him and lean on Him as our source of strength and comfort. And we did.

Our favorite writer, outside of Scripture, put it like this: "Day by day God instructs His children. By the circumstances of the daily life He is preparing them to act their part upon that wider stage to which His providence has appointed them. It is the issue of the daily test that determines their victory or defeat in life's great crisis. Those who fail to realize their constant dependence upon God will be overcome by temptation. We may now suppose that our feet stand secure, and that we shall never be moved. We may say with confidence, I know in whom I have believed; nothing can shake my faith in God and in His word. But Satan is planning to take advantage of our hereditary and cultivated traits of character, and to blind our eyes to our own necessities and defects. Only through realizing our own weakness and looking steadfastly unto Jesus can we walk securely" (Ellen G. White, *The Desire of Ages*, p. 382).

Please, do not feel that I in any way think that my family is above any other. We are not. We struggle with self and sin just as everyone else does. It is only through the grace of God that we made it through this ordeal. Yet, it was only by holding onto the hand of Jesus as tightly as we could that we have not gone into the depths of depression and despair. It is only by the mercies that He has shown us that our eyes have been opened to see His mighty hand moving on our behalf in the midst of this storm. We are not special of ourselves. He wants to draw close to you as He has drawn close to us and as He did for Peter when Peter called, "Lord, if it be Thou, bid me come unto Thee on the water." Jesus said, "Come." He wants to draw close to you as He did with the three Hebrew boys and with Daniel in the lions' den. Christ says, "For I am the Lord, I change not" (Mal. 3:6).

Lawrence began praying, when he was first diagnosed with liver cancer, that God would be glorified. He did not know how God would choose to do it. He did not know whether it would be through his being raised from his illness or through his death. However God chose, it was Lawrence's prayer that God would be glorified. God has been glorified. He gave Lawrence and me a testimony that we would have gotten in no other way.

I did not expect to see Jerold on that Sunday afternoon, and yet he came with the rest of the family to comfort me. His countenance was like Lawrence's had been through those last few weeks of His life. Jerold had a peace and a calm about him that could only be explained by saying that he too was being carried by our loving Saviour Jesus Christ. "For this God is our God for ever and ever: he will be our guide even unto death" (Psalm 48:14).

Jerold and I both have the assurance that our beloved Lawrence and Veronica died with the assurance of claiming the promise of Psalm 49:15: "God will redeem my soul from the power of the grave: for he shall receive me." We both were privileged to see the transforming power of the Holy Spirit in our loved ones' lives. We witnessed the Holy Spirit drawing exceptionally close to them in the months before their deaths. We saw the commitments they made and the laying aside of self that they might be called the children of God.

Oh, yes, we also watched them struggle through the years with the same struggles that you and I face. Yet, we have no doubt that they loved their Lord and Saviour. It was their desire to please God. Jerold and I were privileged to witness how Lawrence and Veronica touched the lives of others with their speech and song. Even more than this, their very lives were a testament to the love of Christ.

In one day, our family's lives have been changed forever. While we were all praying for Lawrence's healing, we knew that, if God chose not to heal him, we must prepare for his death—if there is such a thing as really preparing for someone's death. However, the obvious attack of Satan on our family by taking Veronica the same morning was beyond what we had expected. Nonetheless, we serve a Saviour that has promised to bear all our burdens for us.

"My flesh and my heart faileth: but God is the strength of my heart, and my portion for ever" (Psalm 73:26).

"Thou art my hiding place; thou shalt preserve me from trouble; thou shalt compass me about with songs of deliverance" (Psalm 32:7).

"The Lord is good, a strong hold in the day of trouble; and he knoweth them that trust him" (Nahum 1:7).

"Though I walk in the midst of trouble, thou wilt revive me: thou shalt stretch forth thine hand against the wrath of mine enemies, and thy right hand shall save me" (Psalm 138:7).

"Many are the afflictions of the righteous: but the Lord delivereth him out of them all" (Psalm 34:19).

Yes, God has been faithful to honor His promises to be our strength, our stronghold—to revive and deliver us. He has stretched forth His hand against the wrath of our enemy, Satan, and we have been saved.

There have been many days full of tears for me, and yet, in the midst of these tears, I have found peace in the arms of my Lord. I miss my husband terribly, but I can truly say that I have never felt alone. The Holy Spirit continues to walk with me daily, guiding me, comforting me, and holding me. He continues to open my eyes so that I can see Him moving in my life.

CHAPTER 8. *Encouragement*

During this journey, Lawrence and I received many cards, phone calls, and emails from family, church members, and dear friends. I read every card and email to Lawrence, and he received much comfort from them. During the early morning hours on September 9, a dear friend of ours, Pastor Warren Muir, was impressed to send an email. He did not know that Lawrence was taking his last breaths at the time he sent the email. I did not look at my emails for several days after Lawrence's passing, but, when I did, this is what I found. I was not able to read it to Lawrence as I had all the others, but I would like to share it with you.

Dear Brenda and Lawrence,

The final battle is on. Brother Lawrence, I am happy to know that you are at peace with Jesus. Do not fear death, my brother, if that must be your lot.
I love you, Lawrence, and what matters most now is that Jesus loves you and you love Jesus in return. If you must fold your arms across your chest and await the personal call from Jesus, then lie down as having been a faithful soldier to Jesus.

It is true that, if this life continues for a while yet, we must all die. Death, then, is no bother to the believer in Jesus, for even death has been conquered by that holy Master.

Thank God that you serve One who has power even over death, our final enemy. Press on in strong faith to the finishing line, brother. The Lord has given you three scores and ten! Brenda, fear not, precious one! You and Lawrence have fought a good fight this far. Do not lose courage now. Just as Jesus has taken care of you even through the sweetness of your dear Lawrence, He will continue to take care of you. If that brave husband of yours must go to sleep, then let him sleep off in Jesus.

This is where our faith in Jesus Christ, the "Star of Jacob," helps us tremendously. Thank God for the promises written in the Bible.

Lawrence, pray for Brenda some more. Brenda, do not worry for Lawrence. It is actually more like Lawrence to be more worried for you. If Jesus allows Lawrence to pass off into death, then Brenda, you and I are the one with more trials to face and difficult battles to win. Jesus will make us ready too.

Eternity is clearly in view. Goodbye, my friend Lawrence, if this is the last you must hear from me. I love you, and, though I rarely do this, my face is wet with tears, and I will miss you. Hold that faith in Jesus till the last breath/consciousness is gone from you. Hold those promises of Jesus firm to the end. By God's grace, I will be looking for you in the first resurrection! See you then, if not before!

Warren, Resha, Abigail, Hannah, Jessica, Merlene, and Ceta!

I can never ever repay my debt to the Father, His Son, and the Spirit for the love that they have shown me. It was not by chance that my husband was taking his last breaths as this email was being sent. These words came through Pastor Muir, but they were from my Father. A never-ending love story—that is what God wants our lives to be with Him! There is nothing He cannot and will not do for our eternal salvation. We have only to surrender to Him; He will do the rest. Such wonderful, tender, and loving words of comfort He sent me through Pastor Muir!

Lawrence told me several weeks before he died that he regretted that he had not chosen to speak for God on so many occasions. There were many times that he had been asked to speak to the congregation at our church and other surrounding churches, yet he had declined. He allowed self to get in the way. He never felt that he was qualified. Lawrence knew that he had not taken God at His Word when He said, "My bidding is your enabling" (see Phil. 2:13; 4:13). Lawrence said that, if God chose to raise him from this illness, he would not stop talking. He would take every opportunity the Lord gave him.

It is very important for us to remember that we can do nothing without Christ Jesus. If Christ has opened a door for us to serve Him, to witness for Him, and to speak of His tender love and mercy, we must act while we can. Jesus said: "I must work the works of him that sent me, while it is day: the night cometh, when no man can work" (John 9:4).

> *It is very important for us to remember that we can do nothing without Christ Jesus. If Christ has opened a door for us to serve Him, to witness for Him, and to speak of His tender love and mercy, we must act while we can.*

Lawrence did not get to preach another sermon, but God gave him something more—through Lawrence's death, God has been glorified. Many have been drawn to the feet of Jesus through Lawrence's example of trusting in Christ as his Lord and Saviour. Because Lawrence chose to accept God's decision, regardless of what it would be, many people have longed to have the same trust in our Saviour.

A Symbol of God's Presence

It was Monday morning. Lawrence's memorial service took place on Sunday. All of the family had to leave and return to their regular lives. My son had to get back home as well. He convinced me to spend the night with Valinda, a close friend of mine in Chico. He did not want me to be alone that night.

Monday morning, after leaving Valinda's, I knew that I must resume my responsibilities. There were several supplies running low at the care home, so I decided to stop at the store before returning home. As I drove into the parking lot of the grocery store where Lawrence and I routinely did our shopping, I began to cry. It was as if someone were taking my breath from me. I was unable to get my composure so I walked the parking lot for what seemed to be over an hour, crying out to God for help. I could not breathe; I could not breathe. Again, Christ came to me. Peace began to fill my being, and I was able to resume my activities.

The next several days were very difficult for me. Missing my husband so much, all the things that I had to do, which were things that we had done on a daily basis together, seemed to have no meaning. The activities felt so empty. As I listened to my entries on the recorder for that week, my voice seemed to have no life in it. I recorded these words: "I know God will give me purpose and meaning in my days soon. Everything seems so strange."

As the week went on, I could not stop going over things in my mind. Did Lawrence know just how much I loved him? Did I kiss him enough? Did I do all that I could for him during his last days in this world? Most of all, on the Friday night before his death, when he told me just before going to bed, "God is answering my prayer," did he need to talk to me about dying, and I was not able to pick up on it or handle talking about it? So many questions I had. We are told in Scripture that Satan is the "accuser of our brethren" (Rev. 12:10). I realize now that it was he who was putting all of this self-doubt into my mind. However, I was at such a weakened state from grief that I could not recognize that it was Satan who was causing me to doubt myself.

I had already made plans to spend several weeks with my son in Los Angeles. Yet, I was not scheduled to leave until the first of the month. This week had been so difficult for me that I called my son and told him I needed to come now. I could not wait.

I was scheduled to leave on Sunday, and it was now Friday. I was not sure if I had taken care of everything that I needed to do before leaving, so I decided to sit at my computer and make a list of things to do before I left for Los Angeles. As I sat at the table, I looked out the sliding glass door that leads to the deck and was amazed to see what I believed was a white dove resting on my swing. I am from the city and don't know one bird from another. However, I have seen pictures of doves, and this bird looked very much like what I had seen. I have lived here for over ten years and never have I seen a bird of any kind resting on my deck. I remember one bird flying around for a few moments once. On another occasion, I saw a bird on the railing for a while, but never before had I seen a white dove. Not only was it a white dove, but it was a white dove with great peace and contentment. I began thinking: *If this is indeed a white dove, could this be a sign from God? He knows what I have been going through all week—the questions I have had, the emptiness I have been feeling. Could He be sending me a sign of comfort?* My daughter Nichole came in, and I asked her to go over to the door and open it to see if the bird would fly away. She opened the sliding door, and the bird did not move. It did not even ruffle its feathers. She then began opening and closing the screen door. Still the dove rested on the swing peacefully. My daughter then walked out onto the deck and began taking pictures of this beautiful white bird with her phone camera. Still, the bird continued to rest on the swing ever so peacefully. The whole time I was thinking: *What could God be trying to tell me?*

My daughter had to leave, and, as she was leaving, a friend of mine from church, Regina, stopped by to drop off some papers. As she walked across the living room to where I was sitting, she caught sight of the bird. She stopped in her tracks and gasped: "A white dove—you have a white dove on your deck!" Then she said, "I have goose bumps. God must be sending you a sign!" I told her that I wasn't sure if it was a white dove. She assured me that it was. I then told her that I had just told my daughter Nichole that I was wondering if God were sending me a sign. As she sat down, we talked about the dove on the deck for a few moments, and then I told her that I really appreciated the words that she had spoken at Lawrence's memorial service. She had said that she wanted to tell us what she had observed about Lawrence. She began listing different characteristics. She said that Lawrence was gentle, patient, kind, and loving. As she continued to recite these characteristics, I realized that she was reading the list of the fruit of the Spirit. I continued to tell her how wonderful the moment was when I realized what she was reading and how the fruit truly did describe my husband. I remember thinking that Lawrence did have all of the fruit of the Spirit.

I looked up, and the dove had walked up to the screen door, as if he were listening to what we were saying. We were both amazed. As we spoke of the Holy Spirit, the dove came close to us, as if to listen to us speak of himself. Regina told me that she had to go to work, and she then left.

The dove had now been on my deck for an hour. I sat there pondering what it could possibly mean. After a few moments, I decided to call Lora who lives next door. I told her about the dove, and she began to share with me a story that she had heard about how God used a dog to comfort a lady who was left alone while her husband traveled. She said that she felt God was sending me a sign as well. After I got off the phone with Lora, I sat there for a few moments longer, looking at the bird. Then I decided that I would call my mother-in-law. I explained to her what was happening. The dove had now been on the deck peacefully for two hours. My mother-in-law said that she would take it as a sign as well. She had guests and had to get off the phone. I told her that, even if it were not a sign from God, I would take it as one anyway. The dove represents peace and comfort, and I knew what kind of week I had just come through. I told her that I was going to take it as a sign from God that He wants me to be comforted.

Just as I put the phone down, God impressed my mind with these words. He said, "I sent the dove to my Son at His baptism as a sign of my approval of His life. I spoke these words: 'This is my beloved Son in whom I am well pleased' (Matt. 3:17). I have sent this dove with the same message to you. Lawrence is my son in whom I am well pleased. You are my daughter, and I am well pleased with you."

Again, I must say that God must love me very much to have sent this special sign to me during my deepest sorrow. I was overwhelmed with grief and doubt. God knew that it would take something this miraculous to break through the cloud of darkness that Satan had covered me in. Because I was journaling all of my experiences with God during this time, as He had asked me to do, I immediately began journaling at my computer what had just happened. I did not want to forget the words that God had just spoken to me. I knew that, if I did not record it right then, I might add to what He had said or forget something significant. I wrote it down immediately.

I am amazed that God would, in the midst of managing the universe, come down to me in the form of a dove and speak to me. How tender, how loving, and how kind He is! What peace, love, joy, goodness, and faithfulness He has revealed! God shows nothing but self-control when dealing with us. I felt the full fruit of the Spirit present with me as the dove rested on my deck.

After recording on my computer what had just happened, I sat for a few moments watching the dove walking around the deck. It had now been at the house for over two hours. It was Friday, and I had a few more things to do before sunset, so I got up and went downstairs to place something on the elevator. As I walked past the second level, I saw my brother-in-law in the living room. I stopped and told him, "You are not going to believe what has just happened!" Then I told him about the white dove and the words that God had just impressed upon my mind. By that time, we were both in tears. I told him that, when I left to come downstairs, the dove was still on the deck.

I went back upstairs, and, amazingly, the dove was still there! Those who know me know that I do not do well with bugs or animals of any kind. However, I had to go onto the deck because I have a small freezer on it, and I needed to get something out of the freezer for Sabbath. I hesitated for a moment, but then I realized that I was not afraid of this bird. God had just told me that He had sent it. I went onto the deck, reached into the freezer, and dug around to find the item I was looking for. As I turned around to go back into the house, I realized that the dove had walked right up to my feet and was peacefully standing beside me. I looked at the dove in amazement and joy. I said to the dove, "I want to thank you for being obedient to the Father," and then I went back inside the house.

I realized that I needed to run an errand, but I did not want to leave my house. I wanted to stay close to *my* dove. It had now been on my deck for three hours, and I knew that I had to go now or the Sabbath hours would come without my being ready. When I returned, the dove was gone as suddenly as it had arrived.

I spoke with my friend Regina later that day and told her that the dove had stayed with me for three hours. The next day, when I saw Regina at church, she told me that she had given those three hours a lot of thought and that she thought the dove stayed for three hours because three represents the Godhead. Certainly the Father, Son, and Holy Spirit have each shown their love to me.

We serve such a loving God. I do not deserve His love, and yet He gives it to me freely. He loves you as well. You have only to ask Him into your life. Seek to be intimate with the Saviour. Draw near to Him as He draws near to you.

God has promised never to leave us alone—never. God kept that promise to Lawrence and me. He walked with us moment by moment, day by day, as we took this journey. It is Lawrence and my hope that our sharing of this journey with you will help you to see that we truly serve a God of love and mercy. It was never His intention that we suffer as we do. We can trust the Scriptures when they say, "Greater is He that is in you, than he that is in the world" (1 John 4:4). We do not have to fear—God will always guide our paths. We only have to stay close to Him and listen for His voice. I know that my life is in His hands and that He has a plan. In His time, He will reveal that plan to me.

Chapter 8. Encouragement

As I write, it has been five months since Lawrence's death. Satan has tried to put thoughts of doubt into my mind, and yet, each time the Spirit whispers in my ear, "Remember the dove. Remember the dove." With that encouragement, I am able to tell Satan to flee. I continue to miss my husband. As the days and weeks pass, I come across papers that Lawrence wrote on. Seeing his handwriting touches my heart and brings sadness. However, the sadness only lasts for a moment. Sometimes I hear a song that I know meant a lot to him and tears come to my eyes. Yet, they too are only for a moment. Sometimes I am sitting in the house and all is quiet, and I find myself saying, "I cannot believe that I am here alone." Yet, in all of this, I give praise to my heavenly Father, for these are but fleeting moments. I miss my husband so much, yet I can truly say that I have not felt alone for one moment. God has been faithful. He has not left me alone, and for that I am truly thankful.

My prayer is that I will continue to be strong as my husband counseled me to be while we were waiting in the doctor's office two days before his death. I have always striven to be with Christ for eternity, but now I have another promise that I want to keep as well. I told my husband that day in the doctor's office that I would be there when Christ called him from the grave. As he took his last two breaths, I promised him, "I'll see you when you wake up. I'll see you when you wake up."

O God, keep me from falling. Save me for your kingdom. Remember me.

"...God is love" (1 John 4:8 KJV).

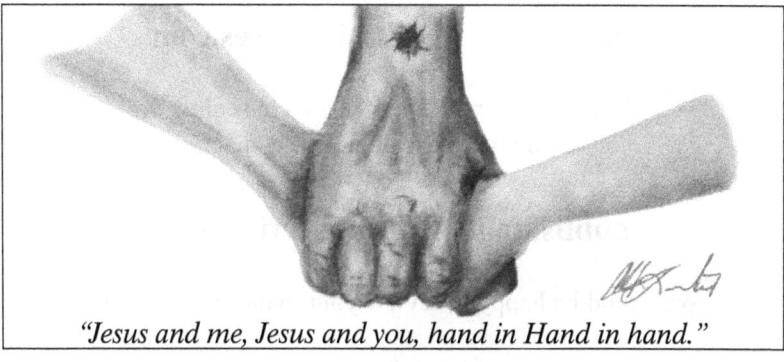

"Jesus and me, Jesus and you, hand in Hand in hand."

We invite you to view the complete
selection of titles we publish at:

www.TEACHServices.com

Scan with your mobile
device to go directly
to our website.

Please write or email us your praises, reactions, or
thoughts about this or any other book we publish at:

info@TEACHServices.com

TEACH Services, Inc., titles may be purchased in bulk for
educational, business, fund-raising, or sales promotional use.
For information, please e-mail:

BulkSales@TEACHServices.com

Finally, if you are interested in seeing
your own book in print, please contact us at

publishing@TEACHServices.com

We would be happy to review your manuscript for free.

www.ingramcontent.com/pod-product-compliance
Lightning Source LLC
Chambersburg PA
CBHW070544170426
43200CB00011B/2549